IF YOU HAVE TO CRY, GO OUTSIDE

IF YOU HAVE TO CRY, GO OUTSIDE

AND OTHER THINGS YOUR MOTHER NEVER TOLD YOU

KELLY CUTRONE

with MEREDITH BRYAN

HarperOne

An Imprint of HarperCollinsPublishers

HarperOne

HarperCollins books may be purchased for educational, business, or sales promo-
tional use. For information please write: Special Markets Department, HarperCollins
Publishers, 10 East 53rd Street, New York, NY 10022.

HarperCollins Web site: http://www.harpercollins.com

HarperCollins®, ®, and HarperOne™ are trademarks of
HarperCollins Publishers

FIRST EDITION
Interior design by Laura Lind Design

Library of Congress Cataloging-in-Publication Data is available upon request.

ISBN 978–0–06–193093–5

10 11 12 13 14 RRD(H) 10 9 8 7 6

For Ava,
my mother,
and the
Universal Mother

CONTENTS

ARE YOU THERE, BABE?
IT'S ME, YOUR SOUL

This is how you've been imprinted to use your relationship to power—to use it against yourself. Every day we create reality based on what we've been programmed to believe. So we spend most of our lives not really thinking clearly and coherently —not initiated thought. We spend a great deal of our lives not really living, but existing in programmed, reactive belief that we call thought.

We can blame the oppressor, the predatory mindset, we can blame it forever and it doesn't mind. It doesn't care.

We need to use our energy, our intelligence in an alternative way to the way we have been using it.

—John Trudell

I was a sophomore in high school when MTV debuted in 1981. I remember it clearly because Joe Morris, a college football player who ended up going pro, was our cable guy at the time, and it was he who brought *Video Killed the Radio Star*, MTV's first video, into our conservative Catholic home in upstate New York. My world would never be the same. I was riveted by the VJs, and in fact, I can still name them all: Martha Quinn, Mark Goodman, JJ Jackson, Alan Hunter, and Nina Blackwood (the blond girl who looked like an ostrich). They were raw and edgy and cool, and I loved the stuff they were talking about. They were like portals into a world I didn't know existed, and I immediately thought, *Oh my God, that's where I want to go. I wanna be* there. I miraculously convinced my overprotective ex-marine father to buy me a trip to New York City for my sixteenth birthday on the condition that it be chaperoned by my twenty-two-year-old half-sister, and the two of us set off on a weekend of pretending we fit in, even as we ate in tourist restaurants in Little Italy and, ultimately, fell asleep during *A Chorus Line*.

I will never forget how, in that very first visit, the energy of New York captivated my every sense. It was like I had stepped out of a boring silent film and into the greatest musical of all time, with Radio City Rockettes kicking to the tune of Frank Sinatra's "New York, New York," while seven thousand angels cried: *"Kelly! You are home!"* I was hearing the sound of my inner voice, and it was *not* subtle. On midtown's crowded streets, I felt electric, vibrant, and alive. I'd never seen a place where people from all over the world spoke different languages, where gay people walked down the street holding hands, and where acceptance was king. I sensed a purpose and vitality in people's lives, not only because of how they looked and how they dressed, but by the way they walked and where they were going and how they were getting there. They were doing real things; they weren't just circling the town in their station wagons, slowly growing old. Here the game was on, and if anyone didn't like it, they could just fuck off. I loved that. I had no idea what I'd actually *do* in New York—I had never heard of a "publicist"—but once I stepped out of my first cab in Manhattan, I knew my days in Syracuse were numbered.

More than twenty years later, I live in a downtown loft (to be honest, I still get a kick out of the fact that the elevator opens into my apartment—how chic!); run my own PR company with offices in New York, L.A., and Paris; produce runway shows in London, Paris, Moscow, Los Angeles, New York, and Miami; and pay my seven-year-old daughter's private school tuition on my own. But this isn't a book about how to be a smart businesswoman, because I'm *not* a smart businesswoman. Frankly, I'm not even that smart. What I am is fearless and intuitive. I'm attuned to the sound of my inner voice, and I've been following it blindly for most of my life, without any clear goals. It doesn't speak out loud; it's more like impressions beaming into my brain from my soul. (Only when I visited New York did it suddenly grow its own horn section.) I believe it has known where I was going from birth. I grew up in Syracuse, after all, a town known as the number-one blue-collar testing market for brands like Tide and Nabisco, whose marketing reps flocked to our grocery stores hoping to determine how their products would fare with the most average consumers in America. Girls from my town didn't move to New York and start their own companies; they met their husband at a nearby state university and worked at the mall or as teachers until the birth of their second child, at which point they left the snowbelt for a warmer life in an average town further south. I may have been organizing elaborate neighborhood barbecue fund-raisers by the age of eight and even landing myself on the local news, but no one around me took this to mean I should consider moving to New York to pursue a career in publicity.* Instead, I was encouraged to study nursing. But I knew from a young age that I was special and that something magical would happen to me. It was my journey inwards—the process of learning to listen to and trust myself—that electrified and transformed my outer journey, helping me conceive and achieve things beyond my wildest dreams.

* In fact, most people I know in Syracuse still think I work in *publishing*.

I'm not here to tell you how to get the perfect Margiela wardrobe or the perfect man or the perfect job in fashion. I've had all these things (though not all at once), and trust me, there's a bigger prize to be had. I want to help you awaken to *your* inner voice—the voice of your soul—and I want you to use it to chase your destiny, which I define as the greatest possible outcome for your life. (Your destiny might involve fashion, but it might also involve teaching rehabilitated sex workers in Cambodia.) *Inner voice?* you may be thinking. *Soul? Destiny? I thought this was a fashion book!* Well, fashion's full of trickery, darling. But if you're going to believe this season's Prada boots will make you sexy and powerful, you should at least be as open to the concept that you have a soul and that that soul has a purpose as unique as your fingerprint and eye scan. If you aren't hearing your inner voice, it could mean you're overburdened or not stimulated enough, or that you've learned to shut it off because the people around you have refused to engage it. Perhaps you've had a hardening of the arteries around your soul. I believe the choices we make in our lives and the people and places surrounding us increase the volume of our inner voice, decrease it, or annihilate it entirely.

This book is a call to awaken and celebrate the magic inside yourself. Here's what you need to do.

1. Ask yourself: Is it possible the voices you've been listening to from birth may not have been your own? Can you separate the voices of your parents, your teachers, your friends, the media, and Hollywood from the voice of yourself—your own inner voice?

2. Believe that your inner voice is the voice of your soul—your own unique spark of the Divine (I would like to point out the similarity between the words "diva" and "divine")—and that it knows and wants what's best for you and will lead you to your individual purpose and destiny. (If you're like me, where you're headed may have *no* connection to where you started.)

3. Gather up your courage like an armful of free clothes at a McQueen sample sale and follow your inner voice wherever it takes you.

If this book inspires you to do one thing, I hope it's to take the years when you're young—say, between the ages of fifteen and thirty-five, before you have a mortgage or kids or anything else that needs to be fed—and go balls out on intuition and follow your dreams. Dreams won't always take you on a straight path to destiny, but they're usually related to what your soul wants for you. They'll force you to ask yourself the hard questions, they'll kick your ass, and most importantly, they'll turn you on. Do you want to go live in Spain and ride motorcycles through the mountains? Awesome. Do you want to become the world's most famous clothing designer? Do it. Actress? Model? Go for it. Do you want to become a CIA agent, a rocket scientist, a Playboy bunny, or a lawyer? Please, be my guest. Maybe when you get there you'll really hate it, at which point you'll know you're *not* a Playboy bunny and can cross that off your list and move on to the next thing. Sometimes, if not most of the time, you find out who you are by figuring out who and what you are not.

The only dream I ever had was the dream of New York itself, and for me, from the minute I touched down in this city, that was enough. It became the best teacher I ever had. If your mother is anything like mine, after all, there are a lot of important things she probably didn't teach you: how to use a vibrator; how to go to a loan shark and pull a loan at 17 percent that's due in thirty days; how to hire your first divorce attorney; what to look for in a doula (a birth coach) should you find yourself alone and pregnant. My mother never taught me how to date three people at the same time or how to interview a nanny or what to wear in an ashram in India or how to meditate. She also failed to mention crotchless underwear, how to make my first down payment on an apartment, the benefits of renting versus owning, and the difference between a slant-6 engine and a V-8 (in case I wanted to get a muscle car), not to mention how to employ a team of people to help me with my life, from trainers to hair colorists to nutritionists to shrinks. (Luckily, New York became one of many other moms I am to have in my lifetime.) So many mothers say they want their daughters to be independent, but what they *really* hope is that they'll find a well-compensated banker or lawyer and settle down between the ages of twenty-five and twenty-eight in Greenwich, Darien, or That Town, U.S.A., to raise babies, do the grocery shopping, and work out in relative comfort for the rest of their lives. I know this because I employ their daughters. They raise us to think they want us to have careers, and they send us to college, but even *they* don't really believe women can be autonomous and take care of themselves.

I named my company People's Revolution not because I'm a Communist—a popular misconception—but because I happen to believe the world will change only when we change ourselves. And that starts with finding ourselves. And *that* starts with listening to ourselves: learning to quiet the clamor in our minds and the voices of everyone around us and move toward what feels right—toward the things we know, for reasons we can't explain, that we're meant to do, the things that make us feel alive. It means taking a journey like the spectacular and terrifying and ultimately mind-blowing adventure I've been on for twenty years. I hope that you too will choose to have a journey instead of just a life. Actually, I hope it's a full-on *expedition*. We live in an intense place, and it will never be transformed unless we as women are encouraged to dream and to find and manifest our highest selves. The planet is here for our delight, but it is also here for us to change, to make it the best it can be. It's not just about sleeping and fucking and getting the right dress. Let's *hope* not.

ONE

FIND YOUR TRIBE:
Your Dreams Are Ballbusters,
Not the Yellow Brick Road

AUNTIE EM: Find yourself a place
where there isn't any trouble!

DOROTHY: Some place where there isn't
any trouble. Do you suppose there is
such a place, Toto? There must be. It's
not a place you can get to by a boat
or a train. It's far, far away. Behind the
moon, beyond the rain.

—from *The Wizard of Oz*

It's the Village Girl who will
change the world.

—Kelly Cutrone

grew up fourteen miles from the Yellow Brick Road. No, really, I did: quaint Chittenango, New York (pop. 4,883), has yellow brick sidewalks in homage to L. Frank Baum, author of *The Wizard of Oz*, who was born there. But my journey to Oz was nothing like Dorothy's, except that I too met gloriously eclectic comrades along the way. When you leave home to follow your dreams, your road will probably be riddled with potholes, not always paved in happy Technicolor bricks. You'll probably be kicked to the ground 150 million times and told you're nuts by friends and strangers alike. As you progress you may feel lonely or terrified for your physical and emotional safety. You may overestimate your own capabilities or fail to live up to them, and you'll surely fall flat on your face once in a while. In breaking away from the familiar and the expected, you'll be forced and privileged to face greater challenges, learn harder lessons, and really get to know yourself. But like Dorothy's, your journey will be much easier with a tribe of mentors, advisers, and trusted friends to help you chart your course and to support you when you stumble. There's power in numbers. It takes a village. Say it however you want to, but the truth is that we cannot go through this life alone. Some of us are lucky enough to be born in the vicinity of our tribe; others will have to travel far and wide to find it, as I did. But I truly believe that whoever you are—whether you're a lesbian who wants to make maple syrup in Vermont, a gay Muslim man in the Middle East, or a fashion-following trend-bitch who wants to get her groove on in New York—there's a place for you to fit in. There are towns and cities where groups of people who reflect you and your own inner beliefs and interests live, and there are communities in which you will thrive. There are people we're related to physically, and then there are people we're related to spiritually, emotionally, and socially. The road to your dreams is sometimes dark, and it's sometimes magical, but *The Wizard of Oz* had one thing right: it's ultimately about the journey and the characters who accompany you on it, *not* about the destination.*

Growing up in Syracuse, while I loved my parents, I never saw myself reflected in the world around me, *ever*. I was like a hovercraft, floating from field hockey to pot-smoking to honor society, seeking a place to land or connect, earnestly trying on identities but finding none that stuck. While I had assorted friends, I never had a *group*. I was a promising figure skater for a while, but even that was a lonely preoccupation because, as you can imagine, I had a hard time connecting with blond girls who

---

* My spiritual guru, a woman known as the Mother, said that true joy is in progress.

wore headbands. My destiny was briefly foreshadowed in an electrifying romance at fifteen with a boy named Eric Klein, who had just moved to town from New York City, where his dad had played in a band with Debbie Harry. Eric was tall and skinny and Jewish and wore a Mohawk and safety pins all over his clothes—which, trust me, was super-hot at the time. He was so irreverently and swashbucklingly pirate-handsome that I couldn't believe my good luck—to be stranded in this fish-fry and Friday-night-sports kind of place and have somebody like *him* appear. I soon found myself engulfed in an exhilarating education in hard-core punk, from the Dead Kennedys to the Circle Jerks. Eric's house was full of curious things like Oriental rugs (we had wall-to-wall carpeting), a futon bed (we had Ethan Allen), and granola and tofu (we had Hi-C and Twinkies). The signs that he was free to express himself included an upside-down crucifix on his wall and the e. e. cummings books stacked on his bookshelves. In hindsight, Eric—he insisted people call him by his punk name, Belvy K—was an early member of the tribe of creative renegades in which I'd always feel most comfortable. He and his family were also my first exposure to a type I'd come to know intimately in the future: New Yorkers. It was no wonder I felt drawn to their house as if by a magnetic force field. Belvy was proof that finding your tribe, like following your dreams, isn't always about what makes sense; it's about what your soul needs. As much as we're looking for experiences that turn us on, we're looking for *people* who do the same, whether creatively, emotionally, spiritually, or intellectually. So if you don't have a well-thought-out dream, you can start by figuring out where you want to *go*. If you cannot see yourself fairly or accurately represented in the community where you live—from restaurants to department stores to clothing choices to conversations at the dinner table—and nothing there makes you feel awake or alive, I suggest you start doing some research on some other communities.

When my dad picked me up from the airport after my first trip to New York at age sixteen, I informed him that I was moving to New York City someday. This didn't go over well; it had been a stretch to get him to agree to let me go there for two days. He pulled the car over to the side of the highway and made me get out. "No way in hell is one of my kids going to live in that hellhole of a city!" he bellowed before literally leaving me on the side of the road (where I remained for a good ten or fifteen minutes; today we would call that reckless endangerment of a minor). But I wasn't dissuaded. I graduated from high school and then college, even majoring in nursing like my parents wanted me to, but I tucked my dream safely away until five years later, when I walked into my dad's study and told him again that now I was really moving to New York. "You must be very rich," he said. "It takes a lot of money to live in New York City." Then he called my mother into his office. "Bev, Bev, come in here! Did you know your daughter wants to move to New York?" Of course my mother knew; she knew everything before my father. In fact, she was a protocol thermometer indicating the best way to approach him with difficult matters. (Sometimes her advice would be, "We're not approaching him at all.") In this instance, she had instructed me to be soft, to explain to my dad how important moving to New York was to me, to ask for his blessing, and to demand nothing. This strategy didn't immediately work: "She can't even handle herself, Beverly!" my father shouted. "You've done her laundry her whole life!" He mocked my meager life savings of $484. ("I can't believe that's all you've saved in four summers of working! You have a closet full of clothes!") Then, finally and somewhat astonishingly, he got out his checkbook and wrote me a check for $2,000. This was an incredible amount of money for him at the time. I knew this, and I started crying. "I love you dearly. You're my daughter, and I would do anything for you," he said, tears forming in his eyes too. "However, as long as you choose to live in that city, I will never give you another dime. If you want to come home, all you have to do is call me, and I will come pick you up and bring you back, no matter what." And that was it. I understood the beauty of his gesture and how hard it was for him to look me in the eye and see me off to a city that fundamentally terrified him. Both my parents seemed convinced I'd come back raped or murdered; it was bad enough that I was already clearly becoming a liberal. But I'd tried things their way, and I was *done, done, done.* Like many parents, mine really thought they had my best interests in mind; they had no idea they were attempting to squash my destiny. You'll find as you set out after your dreams that most people don't really want you to transcend the situation you were born into. Perhaps they're scared for you, perhaps they don't believe in you, or perhaps they're just nasty, negative naysayers. Whichever it is, I advise you to stop sharing your dreams with people who try to hold you back, even if they're your parents. Because, if you're the kind of person who senses there's something out there for you beyond whatever it is you're expected to do—if you want to be *extra*-ordinary—you will not get there by hanging around a bunch of people who tell you you're not extraordinary. Instead, you will probably become as ordinary as they expect you to be. We have a saying in New York: when you're the most happening person at the party, it's time to leave.

It was 1987 when I packed my wardrobe in black Hefty bags, stuffed them into my red Toyota Corolla, scribbled directions on the back of an envelope, and set off on Highway 81. I sincerely believed I was equipped for life in the big city, which was, on the one hand, a nod to the confidence my parents had instilled in me and, on the other hand, total and utter delusion. The place I was headed toward bore no resemblance to the groovy urban utopia I'd been picturing all those years. I'd taken an apartment unseen on Avenue C in the East Village, which in the late eighties was *not* boutiques and noodle shops; actually, it was a Puerto Rican ghetto.* I often felt that the only thing protecting me in my early days there was my black hair, which made me imagine I could maybe pass for a girl from the neighborhood. I soon learned that many of the things my parents insisted on could get me killed: saying "please" and "thank you," for example, only held up the subway token line and caused the people behind me to yell. And none of the transit workers wanted to hear it. They'd just roll their eyes, as in, *Where the fuck are you from, honey?* I also learned

---

* A year after I moved to the neighborhood an infamous pothead named Daniel Rakowitz would kill his ballerina girlfriend and serve her to Tompkins Square Park's homeless population in a soup.

that no one wanted to hear my chatty comments on *anything*: "Hey, how are you?" or "Nice shoes!" or "Do you know what time it is?" No one wanted to help, and nobody cared. That was when I first observed a phenomenon I now call the "New York Slide": you offer your words to try to communicate and connect with someone, but your words just hit a brick wall the person has erected to ward off human contact—the words slide down it and roll away.

But I was a cute girl with a taste for adventure, so I soon managed to befriend the bartenders, punk-rockers, artists, and down-and-outs I encountered in the dive bars I'd stop into for shots of tequila on my way home. (Yes, my neighborhood was so scary that I needed shots to get home.) It wasn't long before I found my way out of the East Village most evenings and into the best nightclubs of the day. It was the late eighties, right before AIDS and crack got out of control and changed New York night-life forever, and an infamous club called the World was still so packed every night with people on coke gyrating and jumping up and down that it always felt like the upper level was about to collapse onto the spiky-haired models and glam-rockers below. It was clear that clubs like this were where the people I'd seen on MTV got their inspiration; *this* was the source, the real deal. I felt immediately like a long-lost cousin of this world. Night-trawlers, party girls, poets, club owners, actors, and riffraff: *these* were the people whose New York lives appealed to me, not the bankers or socialite women stepping out of town cars on the Upper East Side. The people in the clubs worked at night, they had creative jobs, they wore wild clothes; they were like no one I'd ever met at West Gennesee Senior High, except possibly Belvy. I was in awe of them; I desperately wanted them to like me. Still, it was kind of like wanting to be a trapeze artist when the circus comes to town; you're not sure you can swing from those bars.

Luckily, I soon met a woman named Diane Brill, a famed gla-mazon of the nightlife scene who you'd think wouldn't have time for a skinny little girl straight off the boat from Syracuse. She took me under her wing, spiriting me to places like the East Village bou-tique stuffed with drag queens and club kids and owned by Pat Field, the now-famous *Sex and the City* costume designer who was not just the first lesbian I'd ever met but a doyenne of the scene herself. It was Pat who gave me the black Unitard with a push-up bra that would become the staple of my PR wardrobe for years to come. (Later I would wear it uptown with a Chanel jacket and English riding boots and downtown with motorcycle jacket or sti-lettos, all in the same day.) As I formed my tribe, my tribe shaped me. My new friends weren't encouraging me to climb the corporate ladder and make a lot of money, but they were teaching me once-in-a-lifetime lessons about creativity, music, expression, and free-dom of speech (and, ultimately, the price of debauchery). Among them I felt energized, alive, and myself for the first time in my life. And so I went towards them (and still do).

My raging social life had its costs: it cost me my job, for one. I was training nurses for NutriSystem and viewed working for this diet company as more of a stamp on my ticket than an actual career plan. It required me, unglamorously, to make my way to far-flung areas of Brooklyn, Queens, and Westchester to meet with nurses in various NutriSystem offices. Manhattan was hard enough, but in the late eighties the boroughs were a completely different story: grim, desolate, poorly marked, their bridges falling apart. Even Brooklyn was many years from becoming the maze of strollers and brownstone renovations it is today. I'd find myself in the strangest places—GPS and cell phones were not yet invented—with my bag full of rolls of quarters, too scared to ask for help. But that wasn't the only problem. My strict upbringing had failed to provide me with any self-management skills, and my late nights on the scene repeatedly sabotaged my 7:00 a.m. wake-up time. (Let's face it, that was far too early for a future entrepreneur.) One morning, lost and sweating in a subway tunnel, hungover, late to work again and certain I'd be fired, I called my supervisor from a pay phone to say I was quitting.

Rather than look for a new job, I began going out to better clubs and staying there until later hours. I learned that corralling a bunch of cool people I'd met to come with me could get me free drink tickets, drugs, *and* cash in my pocket! In New York parlance, I became a party promoter. And since I was an entrepreneur in my soul, I soon eliminated my overhead, though not on purpose. One Sunday afternoon when an older artist I was dating dropped me off after a weekend jaunt to the Hamptons, I climbed my six flights of stairs to find an eviction notice on my door and all my stuff locked up inside. *Oops*. Party promoting was less lucrative than my former day job, and I was behind on my rent. I never got my stuff back; my possessions were now limited to the contents of my hastily packed weekend bag and my red Toyota Corolla ... which was my next loss. Not really knowing my way around, I'd forget where I parked it, and I was racking up parking tickets.

When the car was towed, I owed more in parking tickets than it was worth, so I never bothered to claim it.*

So there I was, homeless, unemployed, and without a vehicle mere months into my life in the city. I'd been bouncing from one experience to the next, a naive ball of energy and intuition, filled with good intentions (and a dash of the devil), applying myself to everything, focusing on nothing, and making no attempts to curb my appetite for the edge. I lacked mentors, or anyone to call me out on the excesses that were preventing me from charting a course for myself beyond staying out till 6:00 a.m. at nightclubs. Luckily, I did at least have my new tribe of fabulous friends, and though they weren't helping me find gainful employment, they kept me off the streets. I crashed for a few weeks on the floor of the Times Square apartment of an artist named Bernd Naber, a sort of industrialist Andy Warhol who drove a silver Checker cab. Unfortunately, Times Square in the eighties was no less frightening than Avenue C; in fact, it was a human wasteland, littered with crack addicts, hookers, and everyone else who had come to New York with a crime in their head or a dream in their heart and made a few wrong decisions. Every day across the street in the Times Square Hotel a crazy woman would come out in a bathrobe and curlers and walk through the rotating door screaming *"Help me!"* It was a cautionary refrain that echoed my own mounting distress. But I never considered calling my dad. For one, it would have killed him to learn that his oldest daughter

---

* The sad thing about my car was that my dad had saved a lot of money to buy it for me as a Christmas present. Only three years after seeing it parked in my driveway with a big red bow on it, I couldn't even be bothered to get it out of impoundment.

was homeless in Times Square. And to leave New York would have been to give up on the only dream I'd ever had, and the only place I'd ever felt at home, mortal danger or not. Besides, I was naive enough to believe my life was slowly getting better, since I'd now moved *uptown*.

When you're following your inner voice, doors tend to eventually open for you, even if they mostly slam at first. I hadn't lived with Bernd two weeks when the universe sent me an angel. Anthony Haden-Guest, the art critic for *Vanity Fair*, was a celebrated and controversial writer twenty-eight years my senior who was known to have inspired the character of Peter Fallow in Tom Wolfe's *Bonfire of the Vanities* (played by Bruce Willis in the movie). I met him at a backyard cocktail party when he suddenly, out of nowhere, slapped my date—a dashing young advertising executive—across the face, knocking him off his chair, and screamed: "What are you doing with my wife?" It's odd, but we became instant friends. Despite his violence, I found his charisma charming. He offered me the couch in his elegant townhouse on East Eightieth Street, a leafy stretch of the swank Upper East Side. I call him my Colonel Pickering, after the benevolent character in *My Fair Lady*, because despite his status as an irrepressible icon of New York nightlife, he was always generous and gentlemanly to me.* He became my confidant, professor, attentive if infrequent late-night booty call, and one-man crash course in New York in the twilight of its party decade, introducing me to an entirely

* Our arrangement was hard for my mother to understand from afar. So she told my father, preposterously, that Anthony—one of the city's most notorious womanizers, who had once photocopied his penis at a party and distributed it to all the female guests—was gay.

different tribe of people and things that made the city go *BOOM*. It was through Anthony that I eventually met my first husband, and it was also Anthony who finally pointed out the obvious— that I needed an income—and arranged the interview for my first PR job. You could say he was one of the first members of my "tribal council"—a group of wise elders I've assembled over the years to advise me on everything from money to spirituality to how to raise a child alone. My parents never had the answers I needed to navigate my life in New York because they never lived there; they had no idea how things worked. Anthony, on the other hand, had conquered the place and was willing to be my benevolent tour guide. Without him, it might have taken me many more years to get a job, an apartment, and a life.

I advise you to seek out your own Anthonys *before* you are homeless in Times Square. There's a reason human beings once lived in tribes: it's useful. (In fact, I believe the breakdown of the tribal system is responsible for much of the sickness in the world today.) Start by identifying people in your community you look up to and then, graciously and with their blessing, use their hard work and experience to your advantage. Pick their brains. I can't imagine anyone refusing to be a mentor if they're asked in a spirit of sincerity and humility. And if you don't see any of these people around you, do as much travel and research as you can to figure out where they might be waiting for you.

But beware: tribal relationships are a two-way street. As you forge your own tribe, you'll become a member of other tribes and, ultimately, if you're lucky, a tribal elder yourself. This means you'll be compelled to give and give, even when nothing's really in it for you. Now that my days as an ingenue couch-surfer are behind me (I hope), I maintain several floors of live/work space in a large building in Manhattan, and my home has become a temple for an international cast of souls and tribal members needing advice or just a warm meal as they traverse the bumpy roads of their dreams. Lately, these include an Argentinean male supermodel and aspiring actor I met producing a fashion show in Mexico; a friend from an ashram in India who is trying to sell her jewelry line in New York; an employee who is between apartments; my nanny's granddaughters; and even my ex-husbands and current lovers. I cosign leases when my assistants are transitioning from their parents' place to their own apartment; I invite interns to my country house for the weekend; I rush to the bedside of friends' ailing children in the middle of fashion week. I even buy my girls the right lingerie, just as Pat Field did years ago for me. You never know who will end up being your family or where you'll find them. All that matters is that you do find them. After all, your tribe members, whether people gifted to you by the universe or people you seek out and pay, will not only add something unique and essential to your journey but make it much more colorful and fun. These days, my artist ex-husband, now a good friend, may come in off my elevator unannounced to crash for the night while I'm trying to watch a romantic movie on the couch with my current lover and the Argentinean supermodel types away on his computer in the kitchen, and then later all three men may teach my seven-year-old daughter how to play poker. This scene might seem hellishly complicated to an average girl like Dorothy. But not for a tribal priestess in her own temple.

TWO

FAKE IT TO MAKE IT

Faith without works is dead.

—King James Bible

It was Susan Blond, my first boss in the PR business, who predicted I'd be a famous publicist. We were at a record release party at the iconic nightclub the Palladium in 1988, and I was ushering her and Michael Jackson through a packed crowd when she turned to Michael, then her client, and said: "This girl's going to be huge. I've never seen anybody who can get through a room like this." I'd already mastered the indelicate art of using my extended arm as a dowsing rod to part sweaty, intractable seas of people, thereby facilitating safe passage for VIPs. Self-assurance was 90 percent of the game, it turned out; if you act *as if* you know what you're doing, and *as if* you're in charge, you'll be surprised how many people will let you be in charge. This was why, a year and a half after arriving in the city armed only with buckets of enthusiasm and a car full of out-of-date mall clothing, I was leading Susan Blond and Michael Jackson through a crowd of people in New York City. I couldn't believe I was getting paid for this.

Being from the middle of nowhere, I had learned to fake it long before I got into PR, when I was still a club promoter. Homeless and living on Anthony Haden-Guest's couch, I found myself seated at elaborate tables set with several forks and spoons, reading menus offering dishes I'd never heard of, and surrounded by people who were raised in London, Paris, New York, Beverly Hills, Palm Beach, Miami, and Milan. "Where did you go to school?" they would ask one another. "Boarding or college?" another would inquire. "Harvard," "Columbia," "Penn," "Yale," "Switzerland," came the inevitable replies. Meanwhile, there I was, from Syracuse—well, not even Syracuse, but a small town about seven miles *outside* of Syracuse called Camillus, where I'd spent my summers hostessing at Bob's Big Boy. I was beginning to feel as if my past was a curse keeping me from being included. I held my breath during these conversations, not wanting to talk about things I didn't understand or ask questions that might embarrass my date.* I made mental lists of questions to ask Anthony later, such as, "What do people do in Geneva?" or, "What's a venture capitalist?"

My knowledge and pedigree weren't the only things lacking. I'd been raised on Jordache, not Chanel, and my wardrobe mostly consisted of tank tops and the cowboy ankle boots that were popular in the eighties. One night Anthony bought me tickets for a charity raffle at Mortimer's—the infamous and now-defunct Upper East Side eatery then frequented by an international who's who list, including Dominick Dunne, Carolina and Renaldo Herrera, Donald Fagan from Steely Dan, Henry

* Sometimes the best way to fake it is to shut up.

Kissinger, and Richard Nixon—and there I was named the winner of an almost unimaginable prize: a $3,000 shopping spree
at the atelier of Bill Blass (translation: two gowns).* I couldn't
believe it. I knew this was a ticket out of my perpetual outsider
status and a chance to make my horse and saddle match up to
everyone else's. But while the two stunning Bill Blass gowns I
chose may have told the world that I was an urban sophisticate
and I'd *arrived*, it became obvious on one fateful evening that
they were lying.

It was a crisp fall night in New York when I wore one of my
new gowns, an astonishing black velvet and cream satin number with Swarovski crystals striping it, to a black-tie dinner with
Anthony on the Upper East Side. Seated with an Italian count
on my right and a countess on my left, and engaged in a serious
eye-lock with the famous film director Taylor Hackford across
the table, I felt more beautiful than I ever had in my life. I'd only
been in New York eight months, yet here I was, wearing a gown
worth more than the red Corolla I'd lost to parking tickets, my
hair cut pixie-short, my body superthin, seated among people
I couldn't have dreamed up only a short time ago. Standing in
front of the three-way mirror at Bill Blass's headquarters only
days earlier, I'd known I was doing the same thing I'd done since
age three, whether with princess costumes or, later, punk-rock
T-shirts—I was trying on a new identity. The power of clothing
as a communicative medium—a way of drawing things toward

---

* Of course, his check bounced. Anthony was notorious at the time for bouncing
checks, which earned him extra points in his four-year run as the winner of *Spy* magazine editor-in-chief Graydon Carter's annual Ironman Nightlife Decathlon, a competition that also rewarded lewdness and stealing other men's girlfriends.

us or pushing them away—wasn't lost on me even then. Being at the atelier had provided a glimpse of what it might be like to be *that* woman and to have attendants in ateliers waiting on me hand and foot. It felt good.*

Unfortunately, I lacked the experience and self-control to actually behave like the worldly creature I was impersonating, and I soon scored drugs off the Italian count after his wife let it slip during the appetizer course that he was just out of rehab. The count was more than happy to oblige. I assumed he'd given me coke, which people snorted openly from the Bowery to the East Eighties and still do; instead, the bastard slipped me heroin. It was my first and last experience with that terrifying drug, and let's just say it wasn't pretty: after a night spent traipsing to night-clubs and apartment parties and everything in between, I woke up in the morning fully encased in my gorgeous gown with a strange man above me wearing only tube socks, brandishing a whip, and telling me he'd been "a very bad boy." I managed to escape into the bathroom with a piece of the pervert's mail to call Anthony, who arrived promptly to haul me back home—I was somewhere off Lexington Avenue in the Seventies. He wrapped me in his Burberry raincoat and screamed at my captor, in his charming British lilt: *"Don't you evah fuck with her again! I'll have you killed by the Lebanese army!"* We trudged slowly together up Park Avenue, my patient Colonel Pickering and me, my head tousled but my gown perfectly intact. Anthony had saved my life

---

* If finding one's fate is a matter of experimentation, like playing the "hot or cold" game you played as a kid, then this was *hot!* (whereas waking up at 6:00 a.m. to dis-cuss diet plans had been *cold, cold,* very *cold*).

yet again. I felt disgraced, beyond exposed; I'd gone from doing the walk of fame to the walk of shame in a matter of hours. It was becoming obvious that I needed more than witty small talk and the right look to survive in this town. In other words, you can fake your way to the table, but ultimately you have to learn how to eat. Clothes do not make the woman (even if they do make her look *good*).

Anthony said to me soon after, "Darling, you can't do this anymore, you need to get a job." He was understandably weary of me rolling off the couch just as he prepared to draw his bath and go out for the evening. But I still had no idea what to do with my life. It was obvious to me by then that New York was not exactly the meritocracy it's cracked up to be and that, while there were no guarantees for anyone in life, if you were born into a wealthy family there was a network and you'd be fast-tracked. Many of the women I encountered in Anthony's world had attended the same Manhattan private schools, which have names like Spence and Chapin and churn out fashion editors, PR directors, and Lincoln Center board members. (Growing up in Syracuse long before socialites and fashion ruled TV, I'd had no idea these places even existed.) I noticed that these women were not suffering indignities like working at NutriSystem or promoting clubs until 5:00 a.m. I'd have bet that very few of them were washing up on Lexington Avenue in strange men's apartments in their Bill Blass gowns. Their paths seemed straighter, easier—paved. But though I may not have been born on the power-girl starting line—in a hospital on the Upper East Side, with a grandmother on the board at Brearley—I did have one distinct advantage: a very benevolent tribal elder in my corner. When I told Anthony I wanted to be an MTV VJ—I was unable to think of any other profession that really spoke to me—he was unimpressed. "You're far too smart for that," he said. "You should be a publicist." "What's that?" I asked. "It's what you do anyway," he said. "You just talk all day and put people together." He called his friend Susan Blond, who presided over her own firm (and still does), and arranged an interview for me.

I took the subway to Susan's offices on Fifty-seventh Street, and sitting in her anteroom, I was terrified. As I looked through the glass at a well-dressed army of people who arrived at 9:00 a.m., coffee in hand, to do important things all day, I had the same feelings of inadequacy I'd had many months before when I gazed at the excess of silverware at Anthony's friends' dinner parties. I had never known any powerful women, let alone any publicists, and Susan was a revelation; she had long skinny arms and an elegant office with shag carpeting where she sat behind her glass desk with her hands folded, one on top of the other, delivering instructions in a distinctive voice that sounded like a nasal high-pitched bird. In hindsight, she was Popeye's Olive Oyl, as imagined by Karl Lagerfeld. Everything about her oozed chic and power, including the two assistants who manned her office door. And then there was her client list: she represented musicians like the Fine Young Cannibals, Tammy Wynette, the Pet Shop Boys, and Michael Jackson. I was totally out of my league, and I knew it. There was no way to fake it here. But in this case, it was actually my ignorance, not my posturing, that saved me. Susan gave me a quiz, mostly about the music writers at various glossy magazines like *Rolling Stone*, and I got every question wrong but one: what is porthenol? I happened to know the answer to this random inquiry, probably from some extended conversation with my grandmother: porthenol is a kind of lace. (Italian Americans *love* lace.) She was impressed. "Oh, my God," she squawked. "You're the only person who *ever* answered that right. Would you like to be my assistant?"

And just like that, I went from drunk young indigent to salaried PR girl. Granted, I hadn't exactly made it yet. I'd still feel like I was faking it for years. But a road map to the life I'd been intuitively chasing was beginning to reveal itself. I signed on for a scant $150 a week toiling pretty much from 9:00 a.m. to 3:00 a.m., plus Saturdays. My glamorous responsibilities included having organic macrobiotic noodles delivered for the Fine Young Cannibals for lunch—not an easy thing to find in the 1980s anywhere outside Berkeley—picking up dry cleaning, making reservations at the Russian Tea Room, and footing it downtown to Chinatown to see Susan's "doctor," Xu Zhiang, a homeopathic tea maker who didn't speak a word of English and accepted only cash for the remedies he'd prepare for one of Susan's real or imagined ailments.* I threw myself into these menial tasks, never once thinking that I was too good for them or that they were beneath me. I was from Syracuse, after all, and I suddenly *wanted* to be that girl who could walk into a florist and know that long-stem roses were completely un-chic and baby's breath was the enemy, who had a great Rolodex of self-help people at her disposal and knew

* Woody Allen would later mimic this man in the film *Alice*.

exactly where to have lunch with her important industry colleagues. I recognized in Susan the kind of woman whose power
I'd tried on briefly at the Bill Blass atelier (before one of the sales
associates asked me if I'd brought shoes and I was forced to admit
I only owned Doc Martens). Finally, I had a *female* tribal elder, and
a woman whose path could inform my own.

Susan taught me that I didn't want to be just sexy and fun; I
wanted to be powerful. And that just because you're not getting
fast-tracked doesn't mean you can't get on the ride. It's a bit like
Disneyland: if you don't know about the fast-pass lane, you just
have to wait in line for two and a half hours. Is the ride any less
fun? *No!* By the time you get there, it might even be better. The
great thing about coming from nowhere is that you're able to
experience a series of victories on your way to what some people
would consider just a normal job.

Of course, deciding I wanted to be in charge didn't mean I
had any idea of how to be a publicist. When I was finally given
actual PR responsibilities, it was in the form of a record no one
else wanted to work on by a musician named Dan Hartman, who
had years before penned a huge disco hit called "Instant Replay."
His new release was therefore even sadder: he'd had a spiritual
awakening and was aiming to pioneer a new sound called "new
age" music. The record sounded like something you'd hear in a
dentist's office in Scottsdale, and it was suddenly my job to get the
most influential music magazines in New York to write about it.
I knew I'd been given a rare chance to prove myself by succeed-
ing where virtually no one expected me to; the senior publicists
had tossed me this record with a smirk: *Oh, you think you're so*

THE ULTIMATE POWER-GIRL MOVIE LIST

All About Eve
Baby Boom
Belle Époque
Carrie
Cleopatra
The Devil Wears Prada
Elizabeth
Erin Brockovich
Fatal Attraction
Flashdance
Heathers
Idol-Maker
National Velvet
Nine to Five
Species
A Star Is Born
The First Wives Club
Thelma and Louise
Truth or Dare
Two or Three Things I Know About Her
What Ever Happened to Baby Jane?
Working Girl

---

smart, you wanna be a PR girl? Well, here—good luck! Not wanting to waste time figuring out what to do, I just *did*. I cold-called David Thigpen, a well-known music writer and critic for *Time* magazine, and said something like: "Hi, um, my name's Kelly, I'm Susan Blond's assistant, and no one wants to work on this record, and

I don't think it's very good, but there are some things that are interesting about it, would you please come to the reception for the artist, it's my job to get people there?" David and I became friends instantly, and my unorthodox and brutally honest pitching style was born. I realized that writers, who are used to hearing rote speeches all day, thought I was hysterical, and the turnout for the event was fantastic. (The same cannot be said for the album's sales.) Susan was sufficiently impressed to promote me from fetching her dry cleaning to helping promote such records as *She Drives Me Crazy* by the Fine Young Cannibals. Soon I was flying all over the world, staying in hotels with rock stars, and, yes, ushering Susan and Michael Jackson through the Palladium. It eventually occurred to me that I wasn't faking it anymore, at least not as much as I had been. I was being paid to deliver a message for my clients by talking on the phone and attending concerts and parties, which, let's face it, I had a real knack for.

Still, my leap into entrepreneurship was reactionary more than visionary. When I started my own company, I again had *no* idea what I was doing. It all began when I left Susan's to become director of PR at *Spin* magazine for Bob Guccione, who more than doubled my salary to $400 a week. Unfortunately, Bob was sexist and domineering, and after putting up with him for less than a year, I decided impulsively to strike out on my own. I hated that someone like Bob could fire me on a whim. (*That*, to me, felt like true powerlessness.) This way, I figured, if I died, at least I would die at my own hand. But while my inner voice was clearly telling me I was at my core an entrepreneur, it's inconvenient to decide at twenty-three that you can't really work for other people.

Being direct, funny, social, and cute—the traits that had often helped me get by—were simply not enough when I was running the show.* At one of my first red-carpet events for a nightclub, my main area of expertise at the time, I stepped out of my town car to find a horde of photographers waiting for me, demanding to know where the tip sheet was. Huh? *Tip sheet?* I stood there with a confused expression, paralyzed and humiliated, as they unleashed their chuckles and sneers on me. *"Boooooooooo!!"* Yes, I was being booed by the paparazzi! I had somehow yet to learn that a tip sheet is the who, what, where, and when of any publicity event: it provides basic information about the event and its sponsors and the proper spelling of famous attendees' names for the newspaper coverage the next morning (and nowadays the blog posts twenty minutes after the event ends). How had I missed this? I refused to be discouraged; instead, I labored to fill the gaping holes in my knowledge. Much as I had done with Anthony many months before, I sought out older industry veterans and drilled them on mysterious terms like "tip sheets" and "B-roll." And I belatedly picked up a handy doorstop volume known as the *Book of New York Publicity Outlets*, which listed all the writers in the city whose contact information I'd been trying to dig up for months.

Soon all the extra work I put in paid off, and it became obvious that I was on the right track and that publicity was what I was born to do. Mere months into starting my own business, I organized one of the most successful PR events of my career to this day. If

---

* I now suggest working for at least five years in an industry before striking out on your own.

you don't let what you don't know stop you from doing your best in every situation, you will surprise yourself over and over in life, as I have. It started one quiet evening as I stood in my kitchen on Christopher Street making beef stew for my first husband, Ronnie Cutrone, a well-known artist and Warhol protégé seventeen years my senior whom I'd met and married after a whirlwind court-ship while still working at Susan's. An idea popped into my head for a provocative performance art exhibit protesting censorship in the arts. This wasn't totally out of the blue: everyone was talking about censorship in those days. It was a moment when Senator Jesse Helms was taking on the National Endowment for the Arts (NEA) for providing grants for "obscene" and "indecent" art, and Tipper Gore was busy trying to enforce ratings systems on rock music with her Parents Music Resource Center (PMRC). And there *I* was, married to a pop artist who had been a whip-dancer in the Velvet Underground, living on a famous drag queen–clogged stretch of Christopher Street, and moving in a tribe that included people like brash Velvet front man Lou Reed, the aforementioned Pat Field and Diana Brill, Blondie front woman Debbie Harry, and painters like Julian Schnabel and Kenny Scharf. It hadn't really occurred to me before meeting these people that censorship was a problem, since everything in my entire life had been censored. (As a child, I wasn't even allowed to watch *Laverne and Shirley*— too "racy.") But from Greenwich Village the whole world seemed uptight. Who was Jesse Helms to tell people like my husband what was art and what wasn't? According to the senator's standards, anything society might consider controversial—gay issues, sex, porn—was automatically suspect and marginalized. He needed to be answered, challenged, but liberals and bohemians weren't very good organizers. They clearly needed a good PR girl.

My idea was an art exhibit called "Love. Spit. Love." In it we would announce that "*we* [Ronnie and I] are white, straight, married, monogamous, and angry that people claiming to represent us are creating a dangerously false morality." I pictured three couples of varying ages, races, religions, and sexual orientations kissing, caressing, and even having sex in the middle of an art gallery to a soundtrack of love songs from the fifties through the nineties. An American flag would, of course, be prominently displayed on the wall. The idea was fully formed—a direct missive from my inner voice, all but tied in a bow. When I told Ronnie, he agreed that the idea was brilliant and immediately brought a gallery on Lafayette on board to host the show.

Once we enlisted our couples, we set a date—May 1, 1991*—and I went to work publicizing the event. The only tools I had at my disposal were a fax machine, my *Book of New York Publicity Outlets*, and myself. My one-woman company, KBC Public Relations, had never produced an event anywhere near this ambitious before. But rather than worry about the size of what I was taking on, I just busted my ass. I wrote an honest and heartfelt letter explaining why we were doing the exhibit and spent days faxing it all over town. I handwrote a fresh cover sheet for each fax. On the day of the exhibit, there was not one working writer in New York who had not heard from me. I also pleaded with a few low-ranking friends I'd made in television. One, an assistant producer on the

---

* This must be my lucky day: I later gave birth to my daughter on May 1, 2002.

Joan Rivers show, prevailed upon her bosses, and on the morning of the opening Ronnie and I went on Joan's show and shocked her and her audience with news of what we had planned for the evening. Our appearance was the highest-rated episode in the show's history. Censorship was a hot-button issue, and we were basically pounding on that button with a hammer; naked couples having sex in an art gallery drove a certain segment of the population berserk. But we *were* getting our message heard. In fact, no sooner did we leave Joan Rivers's studio than it seemed like every TV show in America was calling us, from the local news to *Access Hollywood*. "Art or pornography?" was the question, and every writer, talk-show host, and cultural critic was dying to answer it. (I happen to think my genius husband had the best answer: "It's art," he said. "Because I'm an artist, and I say it's art.")

The apotheosis of the media blitz came the day after the opening, when, with our pictures splashed across all the morning papers alongside pieces by writers like Guy Trebay in the *Village Voice*, we appeared on *Phil Donahue*—understand, this man was the Oprah of his time—with the naked couples themselves. I'd gone out on a limb and faxed Donahue's producer, who, to his credit, read a handwritten missive from a relative unknown and actually called me. Sometimes you don't even have to fake it—you just have to ask nicely. (The day we appeared Donahue also got the highest ratings in the history of his show.)

The opening itself was the largest art opening in the history of America at the time. The line to get in stretched from NoLita to the Lower East Side, winding through all the corridors of downtown Manhattan; over five thousand people streamed through the gallery that night. I wore a short black wig and pink leather chaps, and Ronnie wore an American flag bomber jacket and sunglasses. In one photo, with our arms draped over each other's shoulders, we look proud and happy. Indeed, the night was an example to me of the magical things that can be accomplished in a true romantic partnership. (I wish I could say there have been many more examples in my life of this phenomenon, but sadly, there have not.) I also learned that you can't fake hard work, and that when you believe in something and truly go after it with all you have, amazing things will happen.

These days, I continue to call members of the media myself rather than outsourcing the work to my staffers, because you can never be too good for the things that first made you success-ful. I will always remember that at twenty-three years old, as an untrained and unknown publicity newbie from Syracuse, I tried my best to get the whole country talking about my message with *no* staff, *no* office, *no* assistant, *no* BlackBerry, and *no* know-how—just with conviction, truth, and balls. And it worked.

THREE

IT'S NOT A BREAKDOWN, IT'S A BREAKTHROUGH

LUCY: You can't drift along forever...
you have to direct your thinking.
For instance you have to decide
whether you're going to be a liberal or
conservative. You have to take some
sort of stand. You have to associate
with some sort of cause.

LINUS: Are there any openings in
the lunatic fringe?

—*Peanuts*

Ego was the helper; ego is the bar.

—Sri Aurobindo

One of my favorite memories from my early years in New York was a New Year's Eve party I threw in the early nineties on the roof of One Times Square, the building from which the ball drops. My then-business partner Jason Weinberg and I invited an exclusive group of editors and celebrity friends to dine al fresco under heat lamps atop the building so as to observe the ball up close before it plunged. When I arrived, the police officers manning the barricades outside at first refused to admit me to the building and couldn't believe that this shockingly young woman in a gorgeous double-breasted silver raincoat from Barney's was in fact the publicist for one of the city's biggest events of the year. But I managed to talk my way past this obstacle, as I had done many times before, and soon I was hosting a dinner party in the sky in an amazing raincoat, my famous artist husband keeping me warm as thousands of people crammed into Times Square below like ants. Several feet away from us on the roof, I was shocked to see eight guys with wires in their hands shouting, "Move to the left!" The sparkling dropping ball, this hyped yearly event that the whole world looks to as the epitome of glamour and celebration and ritual, was really, when you got close enough, just a flagpole surrounded by union workers with cables. It was an apt metaphor for my life at the time, though I may not have known it. Three months later, Ronnie and I were headed for a divorce that left me clutching a bottle of Jack Daniels in one hand and a Marlboro in the other, sobbing and jumping up and down in my underwear on the bed repeatedly singing "Nothing Compares to You" by Sinead O'Connor. But the death of my first love was just one of many deaths I've survived so far in my life. I tell my employees I've died several times while in the same body, each time paving the way for an amazing rebirth (talk about multitasking). After all, you can't truly be happy if you've never known pain. You can't truly feel joy if you've never felt heartbreak. You can't really know what it's like to be filled unless you've been empty. And here's the other thing: sometimes in life seasons don't come in order; instead of fall, winter, spring, summer, we get three winters in a row. (By *my* second winter I tend to feel like a cavewoman frozen in a glacier.) But that doesn't mean spring won't come eventually.

I met Ronnie Cutrone in 1989 at an art opening. It wasn't love at first sight; actually, I found him to be an arrogant asshole. When I asked Anthony Haden-Guest who he was, Anthony said that he was one of those "crazy pop artists." I ran into Ronnie again several weeks later at a club called Carmelita's, but this time he turned on the charm, offering me his coat when I became cold. It was an eight-ball of coke I left in his pocket that finally brought us together. When Ronnie dropped it off the next day with a pint of ice cream, we couldn't keep our hands off each other. (We had sex on the roof of the building.) After that, I immediately began auditioning for the role of his wife by offering to make him breakfast. We moved in together in a matter of days. (By that I mean I moved my stuff from Anthony's to Ronnie's apartment in the West Village.) Several months later, Ronnie said, "I want to marry you." "Great!" I exclaimed. Like most other women, I had been waiting most of my life to hear these words. I was living with a well-known artist in a spacious apartment facing the Hudson River, and he made me laugh. Of *course* I wanted this to go on forever!*

That's how I found myself standing at the altar in a church in Virginia—where my parents had moved after I left Syracuse—in a hideous sparkly sequined dress purchased at my mother's insistence for $300 at an Orthodox Jewish store on the Lower East Side after she'd vetoed the Commes des Garçons wrap-jacket and wide-legged cream chiffon pants I wanted to wear. As a matter of fact, when I woke up that morning in my parents' guest bedroom, "Going to the Chapel" was playing on the radio. It was a perfect opening for the David Lynch movie my marriage would

* The fact that Ronnie was seventeen years older than me seemed totally irrelevant. The fact that he'd popped the question while we were having sex also failed to raise any red flags. Certainly no one ever sat me down and said, "Honey, a young publicist and a much older painter? You don't have a chance in hell!" In fact, my mother, who didn't even know I was dating anyone when I called to share the news, quickly recovered from her shock and took to planning our traditional Catholic wedding like she'd been waiting for it her whole life. (She did suggest we lie to my father about Ronnie's age, but I refused.)

soon become. My hair was curled, and my face caked in makeup. My mother couldn't stop telling me how beautiful I looked.* It was obvious that she'd been programmed to get me married as much as I'd been programmed to get myself married; nothing about my wedding had anything to do with *me* or *my* desires or *my* vision. There I was, agreeing to things like "till death do you part" and "in the name of God" and other things I had no business uttering. What the fuck did *I* know? I was young and impulsive, basically a windup toy charging in the direction I'd been pointed—toward Happily Ever After. I had no idea that there's a difference between being in love and actually being life partners. I hadn't been told that you can make great food together and have all the same interests, but that if you're not working toward a common goal—if you're not actively building something together—there's no reason to get married. In fact, my parents were so pleased with my decision that they proudly staged their own PR stunt, issuing their congratulations on the marquee outside the local Holiday Inn. (Seeing it as I drove into town with my chic New York friends was one of the more embarrassing moments of my life.)

The co-opting of my wedding was the first clue that my fairy-tale marriage, despite the fact that I *did* love Ronnie, was exactly that: a story I'd been told, and someone else's script I was following, *not* something that had anything to do with who I really was or what I really needed at that point in my life. Let's face it:

---

* My mother is a proper 1950s housewife who curls her hair every morning and will not go to the mailbox without her makeup on, so she has never understood why I refuse to dress up and insist on looking "like I live in the Third World."

I didn't even know who I was! I'd made ballsy and intuitive choices in my life, sure, but when it came to love, even I wasn't impervious to the cultural messages thrusting us toward marriage, security, and babies. Only when my marriage crumbled after three years did it occur to me that in buying into all the magical things I'd been told about love and marriage and how to go about building happiness in this life—and I swallowed these notions hook, line, and sinker—I'd built my house on a set of beliefs that were not my own. And a house built on matchsticks will ultimately fall down (though in my case it was more like arson). This was when I learned that you have to give up your life as you know it to get a new one: that sometimes you need to let go of everything you're clinging to and start over, whether because you've outgrown it or because it's not working anymore or because it was wrong for you in the first place. I'd done this before, at twenty-one, when I drove to New York from Syracuse with all my belongings packed in trash bags. This time I wasn't pursuing a dream so much as retreating from one, or several. I'm not saying you shouldn't chase the things I chased—in fact, I still want many of them, minus the Chanel jackets and the husband— but I am saying they are ultimately worthless, regardless of their price, without a knowledge and love of yourself and a firm belief in something greater than yourself.

At the beginning, Ronnie and I were happy. As a glamorous young art wife, I attended dinner parties and art openings and partied late into the night with my husband at Canal Bar, where I'd meet people like Tim Leary and famed Warhol cinematographer Paul Morrissey. But our differences quickly became apparent. I was a young, indefatigable optimist at the top of my game, and Ronnie was a jaded artist who was obsessed with the Yankees and had been inhaling toxic paint fumes for years. As I became more successful at work and more confident and independent, Ronnie began treating me like a naughty little dog that needed training, refusing to let me in when I forgot my keys and at one point forcing me to hire a locksmith and pay $600 of my own money to break into our apartment while he sat on the couch in his pajamas watching the game. He wasn't making me laugh anymore; instead, he seemed depressed and controlling. I didn't know then that if someone's depressed, it's not your fault and there's nothing you can do about it, so I blamed myself for our problems, as many women do. Maybe I wasn't smart enough or pretty enough, or maybe I needed to be more nurturing. I tore through my whole bag of tricks trying to reengage him. But nothing worked. At twenty-four, when I found out I was pregnant, I was thrilled; maybe *this* was the spark we needed. I expected tears, gratitude, and excitement, a loving marital moment—I'd seen this exact scene on TV and in the movies many times—but what I got from Ronnie was paranoia. He said we didn't have enough money saved for a baby (this despite the fact that the man owned Warhols) and that he wanted me to terminate the pregnancy. His reaction broke my heart, and I had an abortion. It was the beginning of the end of our marriage; when I looked at my husband from then on, I just saw a baby-killer. Don't get me wrong: I believe in a woman's right to choose, and I don't regret my abortion—I now know I needed to give birth to myself before giving birth to a child—but it was depressing to end my pregnancy while married and in love. My fairy tale had veered fatally off-script.

Rather than ask myself the important questions in the face of this failure, I threw myself into work even more. I'd taken on a business partner, a former Susan Blond intern named Jason Weinberg, and we started one of the first boutique PR firms in New York, called Cutrone, Weinberg & Associates. I'd been craving a partner who could lend professional support and kvetch with me over the insane people and situations that filled my day. Jason was Jewish, gay, charming, and dashing, and what we lacked in knowledge we more than made up for in attitude. We were soon signing clients like the legendary singer Eartha Kitt, the film director Abel Ferrara, DJ Mark Ronson, Sean Lennon's first band, and every nightclub in New York that mattered, from the Roxy and the Limelight to the Palladium and the Tunnel. This made us *the* kids to know in New York. Actors, rock stars, and hangers-on who wanted to sit at VIP tables and get free booze all night had to go through us, so they all soon had our number. My rising profile on the scene came with exciting privileges like being able to *borrow* clothes from designers rather than actually buy them. I even started appearing regularly in the city's most notorious gossip column, "Page Six," with friends like Naomi Campbell and Justine Bateman. I was a New York girl du jour: I weighed 112 pounds, I owned my own company—for God's sake, I was even in *Vogue!*

And mama, I was miserable. When shit hit the fan, I realized I had few friends I could actually depend on. I knew hundreds of people, but while my tribe was rich and skinny and pretty, we were also shallow; there was no real investment in what was happening in people's hearts and minds and lives. It was as if we'd all made a pact to have short conversations about nothing important. I'd air-kiss these "friends" upon arriving at a club after a long day of work and hear about their fantastic trip to Capri, nod at the appropriate moments, ask the right questions, relay the latest gossip. (I probably couldn't have sat still long enough to have an intimate conversation at the time if I'd tried.) Even my job seemed like a joke and a facade. The truth is that the more zeros you add to your paycheck, the more zeros you add to your expenses, until you're running around like a maniac just trying to keep it all going and you have no idea why you're doing it in the first place. I'd been duped. No one had prepared me for the other side of this pretty picture. What happens when you do meet the man of your dreams—and then you get divorced? What happens when you do get your dream job? Then what? You just get a $100-a-day coke habit and work like a fucking dog all the time? Where was *that* book?

My marriage ended with an explosion, not a slow fade. When I told Ronnie I was leaving him, he didn't take it well: he grabbed a German ceremonial dagger out of his closet and put it to my throat. I managed to escape, which is when he called my father and said, "Lee, I'm going to kill your daughter, and then I'm going to kill myself." He subsequently pushed me down the stairs at the office I shared with Jason, who called the police.* I

---

* Ronnie spent several days in jail and we didn't speak for two years, but we're now good friends and I'm the executor of his estate. His last name stuck, even through my second ill-fated marriage, and I now share it with my daughter.

read about this episode in "Page Six" under the headline "Love Slit Love."

At twenty-six, I had the sense that I had already done all there is to do in life: I'd traveled and toured with kings and partied with paupers, I'd seen babies born, I'd seen friends and relatives die, I'd had a career, I'd been deeply, desperately in love, and now I was getting divorced. My only thought was: *Now what?* Am I just supposed to do this on repeat for the rest of my life? I was reminded of the Peggy Lee song "Is That All There Is?" Was life just a mating game where we're out there looking for a partner and then we have 2.5 kids and, if we're lucky, save over $250,000 for retirement and grow older and either get taken care of by our kids or end up in a nursing home and die? It seemed like we were all just chasing our tails: waking up, going to work, fucking, fighting, loving, saying we're sorry over and over and over again. *What* are we doing here? And who am I? What is important to me, and who and what am I serving? These questions consumed me, but lacking any answers, I did my best to escape them.

I left New York for Topanga Canyon, an amazing vortex of a mind-tripping town in between Santa Monica and Malibu, for the ostensible purpose of opening a West Coast branch of Cutrone, Weinberg & Associates. Really, though, Manhattan had become a very small island where too many people knew my business and I couldn't stop haunting the places where Ronnie and I had hung out, hoping masochistically to run into him. One day Jason called me in L.A. and said, "We just signed Tina Louise," referring to the movie star from *Gilligan's Island.* "But she refuses to talk about *Gilligan's Island.*" This was when I really snapped. *I* *don't want to represent Tina Louise, all she's ever* done *is* Gilligan's Island, *I hate* all *these people, I can't fucking take this, I am* gone! I sold Jason my half of the company and sent my assistant Nancy to break up with the guy I'd been dating in New York, a drummer for Rod Stewart, instructing her to retrieve my couch.* And I got high, releasing myself into the grips of a meth addiction. Soon I was staring at the ceiling pondering a compilation record called *Songs to Commit Suicide By.* (My marketing background told me that the day after Thanksgiving would be the perfect time to release this album.)

It was my second husband, a man named Jeff Kober, who would later put this all into perspective: "Baby, you're not having a breakdown," he said, as I wailed about something or other in the back of our car as he drove down the highway. "You're having a break*through.*" And he was right. The accoutrements of my life in New York had distracted me from really knowing myself, and as I plucked them away one by one—the job, the money, the clothes, even my wigs—I didn't know I was being prepared by a force greater than myself for a major spiritual awakening. The truth was that I'd invested years of my life in a series of beliefs that weren't my own, only to be left with nothing—no tribe, no sense of connectedness or fulfillment—when life dealt me a hit. It turns out there can be a fine line between being courageous in following your dreams and being self-destructive in the service of ego, greed, and approval. But then, my mother never told me

---

* When Nancy arrived at his door with her clipboard, he told her he'd always had a thing for "ginger-haired girls" and seduced her. I see that encounter as one final fuck-off postcard from New York—or at least the universe telling me I'd made the right decision.

that if I did everything I was programmed to do and chased all the things I was supposed to chase—and wear, and *be*—without ever developing a true and unshakeable sense of self, I'd crash into a million pieces one day when something went wrong.

The good news is that while Ronnie may not have been my last great love in life, he was my last true romantic apocalypse: the flaming shards of our love ultimately constructed a bridge I used to walk over into the future. This is an important lesson to remember when you're having a bad day, a bad month, or a shitty year. Things will change: you won't feel this way forever. And anyway, sometimes the hardest lessons to learn are the ones your soul needs most. I believe you can't feel real joy unless you've felt heartache. You can't have a sense of victory unless you know what it means to fail. You can't know what it's like to feel holy until you know what it's like to feel really fucking evil. And you can't be birthed again until you've died.

FOUR

THE TRUTH HURTS:
When Did Spiritual Become Equated with Nice?

For those who are afraid of a word,
this is what we mean by "Divine": all
the knowledge we have to acquire,
all the power we have to obtain,
all the love we have to become, all
the perfection we have to achieve,
all the harmonious and progressive
poise we have to manifest in light
and joy, all the new and unknown
splendors that have to be realized.

—Mirra Alfasa (the Mother)

Early in 2009 I met with Ashley Dupre, the former high-end prostitute at the center of New York governor Eliot Spitzer's resignation scandal, as a favor to a friend. Ashley was earnest and sweet, and she was looking for advice on how to redirect the Spitzer media storm toward a music career. I advised her on where to get her hair done and what designers to wear. I also told her she'd been horribly advised for her Diane Sawyer interview: she never should have apologized to Spitzer's wife, because *she* didn't make a vow to her. (An apology for breaking the law and humiliating her mother would have sufficed.) And I invited her to attend New York's upcoming Fashion Week. Little did I know when she arrived at Yigal Azrouel's show several days later that she'd incite a new media storm with *me* at its center. Her appearance in the front row was uneventful; few people even noticed or recognized her, including Yigal himself, who unwittingly took a photo with her backstage. I was preoccupied with plenty of other "delicate" seating issues: a friend who didn't want to sit near her father's former mistress; another friend who showed up with a lover instead of her husband; Katie Lee Joel, then-wife of Billy and rumored lover of Yigal himself; and an army of editors from rival magazines like *Vogue* and *Harper's Bazaar*. Ashley's seating assignment was not the first thing on my mind. After the show, Yigal and I rushed off to greet one of his sponsors, and he thanked me profusely and told me I'd done more for his career than anyone.* But less than an hour later, when he realized Ashley had been at his show, he and two of his associates viciously beheaded me on the telephone. (I like to call myself Mama Wolf; well, this was Mama Wolf being attacked by a pack of hungry hyenas.) He told me he was going to send out a press release immediately announcing my firing. I gave him one last bit of free advice: that that would be a huge mistake. I was on the number-one-rated cable TV show at the time, and my new friend Ashley, well, she'd been involved in the biggest media scandal to hit New York in years. The news would inevitably eclipse any positive reactions to the actual clothes. But Yigal ignored me, blasting a press release to the entire industry that announced he had fired me for "mismanagement." Everyone knew what that meant. By nightfall it had become the scandal of the week.

I cried in my office that night, not because I'd been fired, but because I was devastated by the state of humanity. I knew that the blogs would eventually move on to fresher gossip. I also knew I'd recover from the personal embarrassment of having my name

---

* And I had: I gave him $25,000 worth of free services and pulled in sponsorships that essentially allowed him to show at the Tents for free.

dragged through the mud by one of my own clients at a moment when the whole industry was watching. What upset me most, however, was the hysteria over this young girl who made some bad decisions and ended up in the oldest profession in the world. Could it really be that, in 2009, the fashion industry—which creates images of girls who look like they've been gangbanged on *Alice in Wonderland* adventures and calls them ad campaigns—was turning on me because I gave a front-row seat at Fashion Week to some girl who, like many of the women who attend fashion shows and go to Chanel, had sex for money with a man thirty years older than her? *Fuck that.* When Ashley called to apologize and to tell me I could pretend I didn't know her, I gathered my resolve. "I'm not going to pretend I don't know you," I said. "In fact, tomorrow's Valentine's Day. Do you have any plans?" I brought her along to my client Andrew Buckler's event, where I told a reporter from *Women's Wear Daily*, "We're all hookers in one way or another."* The quote was featured as the 'Quote of the Day' on *WWD*'s inside cover, and as a result, it tore around the Internet. My mother soon called to tell me she'd seen the scandal on three different morning shows. It dragged on for almost the entire week, which was one of the longest of my professional life.

Fashion is an industry built on illusion, and publicity is a profession built on spinning the truth. But I'm a person who has become well known for being honest at any cost, whether that means stoking the fires of my own Fashion Week scandal or

---

* And I meant it: we all do things we don't want to do for money. If you're paying me $20,000 a month to be your publicist and you call me to talk about whether aubergine or celadon is going to be psychically on-trend for the season, nine times out of ten I don't really care. But I'm being paid to do a job, so I give good phone.

telling models that they're too thin. I don't regret speaking out against my industry's hypocrisy, though in this instance and in many others over the years it wasn't exactly the easy road to take. Society wants you to participate in its lies, but I've seen this produce terrifying consequences in fashion, from drugs to anorexia to abusive relationships. We tend to spend our lives building a stable of partners in our crimes against ourselves: people to tell us we look thin when we're overeating, people to tell us we look gorgeous when we're spent, and people to tell us we're making sense when we're not. With friends like these, we're almost put off when people decide to be honest. But *true* friends love us no matter what and are willing to call us out.

That's why, at People's Revolution, when someone comes in on Monday morning and says, "Did I gain weight over the weekend?" her colleagues will probably look up and say, "Yes." And if I grab a studded T-shirt off one of the clothing racks that perpetually clutter our office and ask, "Does this look bad?" the answer will also likely be "Yes." I've had to tell my daughter that there is no way her father and I will ever be married, and I've had to tell clients that their collection is not welcome at *Vogue*; sometimes the truth just hurts. You can either let someone be protected from reality or let them be sculpted and birthed by it. I firmly believe the latter option is best. We're constantly getting these messages to mind our own business and look the other way if we want to be well liked, to not tell the truth or speak our mind or say anything too intense. Well, I'm telling you here that this approach not only makes you party to other people's crimes against themselves but is a prescription for mediocrity and delusion.

Many people are surprised to discover that I'm a very spiritual person. After all, I run a business, I say what I think, and I wear all black; we have words for these things in this country: witch, bitch, and cunt. But the truth is that it's *faith* that gives me the power to speak my truth, and faith that makes me fierce. Being "spiritual" and being "nice" have absolutely nothing to do with each other, contrary to the popular notion that "spiritual" refers only to vegans in Whole Foods whispering to each other. Kindness is important, and the heart plays an important role in the progression of humanity, but I don't believe we should all just get naked and skip in the sun. Ultimately, we need to be able to battle our demons within and without to get where we want to go. Jesus turned over tables and defended hookers, and the Hindu goddesses were *not* messing around. Hanging in my office is a large image of the Hindu goddess Durga, who taught me a lot about spirituality. In her eight arms she bears swords, conch shells, tridents, thunderbolts, bows, and discuses: a weapon for every possible occasion. In the Gita, an Indian sacred text, she annihilates demons, rides lions, *and* makes divine love to her husband. (This sounds to me like the perfect day.)

I'm devoted to my job not because I love it, but because I look at it as my spiritual practice. There is a word for this in India: *karmayoga*. I am a karmayogi—someone who becomes conscious of herself and the Divine through work, not through meditation in some ashram or saying Hail Marys. On any given day I'm not just dressing naked male models or negotiating an appearance by a celebrity at one of my client's events, but figuring out who I am by doing what I do. You can do this in any field, of course, but there's nothing like a superficial industry to really make you want to know God and force you to be constantly rejecting false belief systems and defending the truth. New York, Los Angeles, Paris, London—these are places where lower human energies like greed, violence, and lust are always in play. (In fact, "luxury" is derived from *luxuria*; the first of the seven deadly sins, it literally means "lust.") If you work in this industry and have any clue as to what's going on, there will be moments when you think, *This can't be real—we have not just spent twelve hours trying to get a coconut-shell bikini through the agriculture inspectors at customs when there are sixteen thousand homeless kids in New York City!* If I weren't a spiritual person, I would have shot myself in the head a long time ago.

This circus of materialism and superficiality, however, has forced me to learn to trust and love myself and really know that I'm not what I do for a living. It's liberating to be forty-four years old, standing next to a six-foot model, and feeling no anger, resentment, or jealousy—to be able to appreciate her beauty while also loving myself. And it's liberating to be able to make a true, if incendiary, comment to *Women's Wear Daily* and stand by it rather than feeling embarrassed or ashamed. (I felt bad for my other clients and for the state of my industry, but I didn't feel one iota of remorse for knowing or owning up to knowing Ashley.) In a way, fashion is the karmayogi's ultimate ashram.

Of course, before fashion became my ashram, I was just a girl chasing a husband and a great wardrobe like everyone else I knew. The story of how I became a seeker is as unlikely to some people as the fact that I *am* one. I never really belonged to any religion before I moved to New York, least of all the Catholicism of my youth, but by the time I married Ronnie Cutrone I was a devout member of America's number-one denomination: capitalism and ego. (I'm sure most American households give more money to MasterCard than to their church.) My particular sect was the "Don't you know who I am" club, and we subscribed to several mantras: "I am who I know," "I am what I do," and "I am what I have." I never really considered that I was connected to something greater than Hermes—admittedly, a great thing to be connected to—or that there was something more to me than the numbers in my bank account or the solidity of my marriage.

Often the Goddess starts challenging this kind of complacency with gentle taps on your shoulder, asking quietly, "Do you want some help?" At which point, if you're like I was, you'll say, "No thanks, I'm having a really good time!" Eventually she hits you in the back of the head, and perhaps you again refuse help: "No, get out of here. I'm having a really good time!" Finally she sticks her stiletto in your heart chakra like a pre-op transvestite while putting cigarettes out on your body and demands, "Okay, are you ready to change *now*?" Basically, when destiny calls, we don't always go willingly. I certainly didn't. But after losing everything in the aftermath of my divorce, I had a profound spiritual awakening that changed everything I thought I knew about myself. My life would never be the same.

It happened in the fall of 1992. I was living in the decidedly un-chic Beverly Laurel Motel after being evicted from my house in Topanga Canyon for nonpayment of rent. The demands of my drug habit precluded any sort of real employment, so I'd taken to taping my old press clippings to the wall of my room and folding my clothes in alphabetical order by color to pass the time (amber, blue, cinnamon, dusty rose, evergreen). After selling off my Chanel jackets and other remnants of my life as a top PR girl to used-clothing stores like the Wasteland (one reason it's good to buy designer: if you bottom out, the resale value's much higher!), my days dissolved into a cycle of illusion, disillusion, hallucinations, sleep deprivation, isolation, loneliness, and all the other consorts of addiction. I had joined the underworld of people who are alive but not living.

One morning I awoke to a voice telling me there would be a miracle or I'd kill myself at midnight. *Thank God*, I thought. Then I went about my day, which eventually led me to my regular pit stop, the Bodhi Tree, a spiritual bookstore where I'd go to read about astrology and the cult of Mary Magdalene and where I'd sold books to pay for my motel room. I was sitting on a bench outside the store waiting for my cash when I saw him: a middle-aged man with white hair and a belly, walking toward me. "You better watch out, the moon is going to get you," he said, gesturing toward the full moon in the sky. Something in his tone pierced my pharmaceutical trance, and I started to cry. "Pal, can I get your number?" he asked. For reasons I can't explain, I told this man where I was staying and my room number.

It was past 11:00 p.m. when my phone rang. "Listen, pal," the man said. "I'm outside your hotel, and I have something for you." "I have an appointment at midnight," I snapped. "You'd better make it quick." I was already running the bathtub and beginning to undress, admiring my speed-freak body in the mirror. After several bouts with self-diagnosed anorexia, I had decided I was indeed thin enough for suicide in the bathtub naked.

When the man appeared at my door, he asked me if I was willing to go to any lengths to be in the light. "As long as I don't have to sleep with you," I replied matter-of-factly. I let him in to my room. He was wearing a sweatshirt and looked more like a Vietnam vet than a holy person. He told me to lie down on the bed; then, holding his hands about three inches over my body, he moved them through the air from my head to the tips of my toes. When he was finished, I felt my soul sit up into an erect position while my physical body lay supine, and I started to cry. Suspended in the air above the bed, as clear as day, floated the face of a woman I'd never seen before. She was Western yet also looked vaguely Indian; I thought she kind of looked like me. Her presence was, in that moment, the most real thing I had ever experienced. She was silent, beaming divine power and love with piercing eyes, and her gaze beckoned to a part of me I didn't know existed. I described her to the man, whose name was John, and he nodded. "You're one of the Mother's children," he said. He explained that the Mother had been a French-born guru living in India. Then he wrote down a mantra for me. *Om Anandamayi Chaitanyamayi Satyamayi Paramei.* "Say this in repetitions of three, and grow it like a garden inside yourself," he said. Then he left.

For the next six months, I would suffer nerve damage that left me forgetting how to spell words and occasionally having trouble writing, but that night marked the last time in my life I ever touched drugs. The morning after my vision, I woke up completely sober, left the hotel, and, aware that I had tested my parents to the breaking point, called my grandmother from a pay phone and pleaded with her to send me $500 via Western Union. I used the money to book another hotel room on the corner of Beverly and Spaulding.* The man at the front desk practically sneered at the ghastly sight of me. "This is not a cathouse," he said. I didn't even know what a cathouse was. (Evidently, it's a brothel.) "I'm having a very hard time, and I just want to pay," I told him. He let me check in, and for five days I endured the ravages of a truly horrifying detox. When I went in to the shower—which happened often because I was sweating profusely most of the time—it would appear to be filled with cockroaches. I barely ate. I did a lot of sitting on the floor and crying. Though both were pretty strong, my will to live was slowly beating out my will to die.

I soon ran into a girl I knew from New York who told me there was a club opening on La Cienega Boulevard called the Gate. She arranged for me to do PR for the opening, and with the $3,000 fee I was able to get a one-bedroom apartment for $625 a month. Once settled, I dedicated myself to a life of meditation and chanting the mantra John had written down for me. By this time I had lost or pushed away everything that had mattered to me, yet all I could see when I woke up each day was the sheer amount of beauty flooding my life and the world. There was so much I'd missed by indulging the lower energies of my mind: greed, ambition, insecurity, self-doubt, guilt. As I became conscious of something greater at my core—I couldn't prove

* I'd been told I was no longer welcome at the Beverly Laurel, owing to nonpayment and the constant presence of my drug dealer.

it, and still can't, but I *know* it—a huge weight lifted off me; I experienced the wonders of the world with something akin to childlike awe.

One day as I sat outside of Erewhon, a health food store in L.A., eating a snack I'd bought with whatever scant money I had, my eyes settled on a flock of pigeons. I was totally overwhelmed, transfixed even. When you really look at them, pigeons have all these amazing shades of purple and blue in their feathers. How had I never noticed? I had lived a fast life in New York and soared to the highest highs on drugs, and now here I was, a yogi having a profound experience with pigeon feathers! And all it had taken was giving up everything I had and washing up penniless and near death on Beverly Boulevard! I sincerely hope you don't have to take such a self-destructive path to get to the same place. But for me, it was through this demolition that my new world was built. I realized I didn't need any of the things I'd depended on. I had the whole tool kit already inside me. That day in front of Erewhon I felt true happiness and peace for the first time in my life. And, sister, I promise you that it was better than any drug I've ever taken.

I began wholeheartedly studying this woman known as the Mother who had appeared to me at the Beverly Laurel, reading everything about her I could get my hands on.* From the beginning, her teachings struck me as real and correct and totally relevant to my life. She became my *guru*, which simply means

* I learned that she was a Parisian-born Egyptian Turkish Jew whose life journey led her to Pondicherry, in the south of India, where she met and partnered with the Indian philosopher and guru Sri Aurobindo (who named her the Mother) in 1920. Something of a spiritual power-girl herself, she played tennis and drove a Bentley!

"teacher" in Sanskrit, initiating me into teachings and belief systems from Eastern mysticism and Hinduism to Kaballah and Tantra. I discovered goddesses like Durga, who challenged every perception I'd ever had of the feminine in religion; I began to understand that the Catholicism of my youth is not the only way to know "God." There are notions of the Divine that don't include the man with the thorns and the blood and a congregation of submissive, veiled, silent nuns. In fact, in ancient schools, women had power too and were worshiped equally. Native Americans refer to Mother Earth and Father Sky, and the Hindu gods Shiva and Kali are partners and draw their powers from each other—Kali can't dance without Shiva, and Shiva can't sleep without Kali. These feminine forces weren't just the weaker half of lopsided pairings, quietly riding on the donkey while Joseph figured everything out. I realized that all over the world women are taken to places of worship where they have no voice. Somehow it's even more ironic that we accept this second-class status in the United States, even as we fight for equality at home and in the workplace. This is why I'd instinctively flipped off religion growing up, and why I've refused to raise my daughter in any one religion.

As I set about assembling a set of beliefs that better represented me, my first thought was, *Why shouldn't He be a She?* So I appointed a She as head of my church and temple: the Goddess. (Of course, this Goddess is partnered with a God, her lover, collaborator and equal. We must not eliminate the male; we must embrace each other and transform.) I choose to believe that my soul is a unique and individual part of the divine feminine force in the universe, as is yours. If I had to describe my DIY religion, I'd say that I'm a Hindu-esque Tantric Toltec Priestess, which you've never heard of because I made it up. My religion is not about worshiping the divine at noon on Sundays, nor is my God locked away in a church to be visited once a week. My religion is about manifesting the Divine in myself and in everything I do. For me, the Goddess embodies compassion, perception, ruthlessness, and a total commitment to the destruction of falsity and ignorance; I aspire to embody and be all these things. The Mother remains my guru to this day, and I continue to consult her teachings for guidance. But ultimately my religion is deeply personal. I've used ancient belief systems as a way to dig through modern nonsense and really get at my core: to discover who I truly am and to understand what I'm meant to do here.

I'm not trying to convert you to my religion, or my concept of the Divine. I'm not the Mother's publicist, nor does she need one, and I don't think Eastern meditation is the answer for everyone. In fact, the Mother's spiritual partner, Sri Aurobindo, estimated that there are 64,000 paths to the Divine. What I am encouraging you to do is to think and to question. Too many people believe BMWs are great cars because everyone says they are, not because they've ever driven one. Too many people get married in Catholic churches because their parents want them to, not because that institution provides them with any spiritual meaning. I'm suggesting that you don't have to go to churches that don't honor you, and you don't have to tithe your money to institutions that don't believe in birth control. You can instead appoint yourself High Priestess of your *own* religion, and you can

TWELVE STEPS TO STARTING YOUR OWN RELIGION

To start your own religion, you must be open to the idea that there is no one religion unifying the whole world and that we must step away from strict religious affiliations and envision and embrace a new world where people are allowed to have their own concept of God and the Goddess, where each person is entitled to worship, embrace, and know the Divine without conflict, war, or persecution.

Although starting your own religion may seem like a lofty endeavor, the time is now and you are indeed a pioneer. As a love-bringer who will help transform the earth, human beings, and, yes, even yourself, you are a part of a new truth. Following these suggestions will help you manifest that truth.

[1] Uncover, discover, or recover *your true self.*

[2] Accept the fact that you have been programmed by society, your family, religions, Hollywood, and other influences. Become fully conscious of this programming so that you can deprogram yourself and resist what society has been demanding of you.

[3] Forge an unprecedented alliance with yourself. Most people don't have an intimate relationship with the caring voice of knowingness that is actually a part of each one of us. *The Divine lives in you. You are divine.*

start by examining what it is you're already worshiping. If you're in a store spending all your rent money on a single article of clothing, awaken to the idea that there might be a better church for you than Gucci. Book a trip to Oaxaca, Mexico, or Machu Picchu or Stonehenge or Paris or the Grand Canyon or any number

[4] Study as many spiritual texts as you can, including philosophers from Plato to Tolle, Sri Aurobindo, Amma, Castaneda, and beyond.

[5] Attend different churches, temples, and synagogues and worship with everyone from Sufis to Muslims to Catholics to Jews.

[6] Take what you like from each religious tradition you encounter—in other words, *what resonates with you*—and leave the rest.

[7] Weave all of your truths together, then piece together one big quilt of your true beliefs.

[8] Ask yourself why anyone would place God in a building to be visited at their leisure. Promise yourself that you will never do this with your religion. *Incorporate conscious contact with the Divine into your daily life.*

[9] Be open to new lessons.

[10] Tell the truth no matter what.

[11] Let the truth be expressed in your life at this moment with abundant and balanced energy.

[12] Celebrate and cultivate the health, strength, beauty, and ease of your physical body. Be happy in your body.

of other sacred places around the world. Study as many religions and teachings as possible; take what you like from each and leave the rest. Visit a mosque, a chapel, a temple, an ashram, and while you're there read the great texts. Women should spend as much time looking for a religion of their own as they do trying to find a hot guy to have sex with. Because let's be honest: there are too many examples of magic and miracles in this world to say with any certainty that there isn't something fantastically wonderful going on here. The searing emptiness I felt after my divorce taught me one thing, and it was one more thing my mother never told me: if you don't have faith in yourself and in something larger than yourself, and if you want to take this world at face value, you're going to have a fucking nasty ride.

Perhaps you're wondering how I went from blissed-out yogi in L.A. to overtaxed—I mean this in more ways than one—fashion publicist in New York. As the days of my detox churned into a spiritual awakening, I received what I can only describe as a cosmic installation giving me the ability to read tarot cards. Luckily my entrepreneurial spirit was still intact, so I took my new gift to Venice Beach, where I gave readings to tourists, Angelenos, and freaks on the boardwalk every weekend. Whatever compelled me to take the hour-long bus ride from West Hollywood to Venice Beach that first day, I can't really explain; it *must* have been a force greater than myself. But as my readings got better and I turned up the charm, my business grew, and soon I had private clients. The business that started out with $10 donations on the boardwalk grew to $120-an-hour consultations in my apartment in West Hollywood. I even supplemented my income by chatting on the phone for $3.99 a minute on the Psychic Friends Network.

Meanwhile, I took my first tentative steps into the fashion business. I started going out to thrift stores in the Valley to buy interesting pieces of clothing priced at $4.25 that I could flip for $15 at the Wasteland, the same vintage and resale store where I'd desperately pawned my Chanel jackets for $50 not so long before. I was just trying to eat, but as a natural kar-mayogi, I couldn't help but pour my heart into my work, and my side businesses were soon flourishing. Totally by coincidence, I received a call one day from one of the owners of the Wasteland. He was looking for someone to do his PR, he said, and he'd heard that I was a publicist from New York. Was I interested? I found it mildly devastating to consider representing a used-clothing store on Melrose when I'd formerly worked with people like Frank Sinatra, but the Wasteland was offering me $3,000 a month, which I couldn't refuse. It was certainly a lot more than my fledgling resale operation would ever bring in. I turned again to the teachings of the Mother, who advocated getting off the ashram, so to speak, and taking not just your knowledge and peace and joy but your character defects as well—in other words, your whole self—out into the streets. *Then* we'll see what you're made of, she said; *then* we'll see who's spiritual. (Her teachings echoed the exhortations of my actual mother, for whom watching me make my living on the Venice Beach boardwalk had been almost as terrifying as witnessing my descent into drugs. "You can't keep living like this!" she'd blurt out when we spoke.)

From the Wasteland job, my career took off quickly. No sooner had I begun working out of an office in the back of the store than a friend called me up saying that she knew a woman who wanted to sell her vast collection of vintage Pucci and did I know anybody who might want to buy it? In fact, I *did*. I arranged for my clients at the Wasteland to purchase the collection, branded it "The world's largest collection of vintage Pucci" and arranged a party, a fashion show and a sale, which tripled the store's revenue in under one month. I also secured a feature story on the front page of the *Los Angeles Times*. Encouraged by my success, I went on to snag the store a three-page feature in *Vogue* that focused on its celebrity clientele. The Wasteland was a local L.A. phenomenon no longer—and I was officially a publicist again.

Next, I signed the Sunset Marquis Hotel, and soon after that Deepak Chopra came calling. "Shut up," I told my assistant when she came in to tell me he was on the phone. "Take a message." I certainly did not believe that Deepak Chopra was calling me—but I was wrong. He'd gotten my name through a mutual acquaintance, and he and Rasa Records owner Donna D'Cruz wanted me to do PR for his new record, which featured people like Demi Moore, Madonna, and Goldie Hawn reading the poems of Rumi. Just like that, I went from reading tarot cards on the boardwalk to counting one of the most famous spiritual figures in the country among my clients. The flower was in bloom; I was an up-and-coming power-girl entrepreneur yet again.

This time, however, I was determined to do things differently. My business pursuits weren't exempt from my divine aspirations to show compassion and destroy falsity (even though, as with any yoga practice, I would have to keep making these efforts for years before they really came naturally). I wasn't just accumulating status and possessions, as I'd done in my early twenties. I now knew that I am ultimately here to take in the adventure of life and to know and express my highest self and best qualities, thereby doing my part to transform the earth. This knowledge almost always makes my course of action clear.

For instance, when I saw a man violently hit his child at an airport in Mexico recently, I walked right up to him and told him he was a monster while fifty other adults stood around thinking, *Gee, I'm kind of uncomfortable about this* (I'd like to stress that I was in an international terminal full of people from all over the world). Guess what? You're also implicated. All of us are taught to sit back and just watch this sort of thing when it happens. But ask yourself: Why do you act, or not act? Who are you defending? What are you doing here on this earth? My odyssey in the years since my vision has repeatedly tested everything I learned about myself in my days as a yogi, forcing me to slay demons again and again, but I look at every challenge and mistake as an opportunity to progress. And most of the time my beliefs steel me with the power to speak my truth and take responsibility for it. *This*, to me, is true freedom.

At first I thought young women would be afraid of me because of how harshly I'm portrayed on television, but when I meet them walking around my neighborhood or traveling to L.A. or flying to London for London Fashion Week, they all want to know how they can be power-bitches too. They want to own their own companies and be truth warriors and achieve the same freedom I've fought so hard for. I believe all women know in their heart of hearts that they truly are divine and magical, even if they've temporarily forgotten. Speaking the truth has made me some enemies. But it has also gotten me much further than I would have otherwise progressed in life. Let's face it: being nice does not always remove obstacles, and in fact sometimes it creates them. That's why, the next time you hug someone you secretly despise and say, "It's great to see you," I want you to bite your lip. You don't have to say anything you do not mean, and I urge you not to. The night I was fired by Yigal Azrouel, while I was still reeling from my industry's prudish and hysterical reaction to Ashley Dupre—I mean, let's face it, this girl would've been on her way to being a huge star by now in Europe!—I called another of my clients, Jeremy Scott, and told him to make me a T-shirt that said, WHAT WOULD MADONNA DO? "Oh please, I don't need to make you a T-shirt," Jeremy replied. "Madonna would've grabbed that girl by her ponytail, made out with her, and said, 'Why are you talking about my girlfriend like that?'" Suddenly I realized that I hadn't maximized my moment.

FIVE

WORRIER TO WARRIOR

The spirit of a warrior is not geared to
indulging and complaining, nor is it
geared to winning or losing. The spirit of
a warrior is geared only to struggle, and
every struggle is a warrior's last battle
on earth. Thus the outcome matters very
little to him. In his last battle on earth a
warrior lets his spirit flow free and clear.
And as he wages his battle, knowing
that his intent is impeccable, a warrior
laughs and laughs.

—Carlos Castaneda

If anyone really wanted to change the world, they'd bring in the fashion bitches, because nobody gets things done faster. If we went about saving the world like we go about producing fashion shows, well, let's just say New Orleans after Katrina would've been fucking *sorted*. (We'd all have been wearing Paul Smith wellies and barking, "What do you mean your head's bleeding? Get up, let's go, *move!*") My experience in the fashion industry has taught me to act confidently and decisively, without regret or self-doubt—in other words, with detachment from the outcome, which is the end goal of any good yogi. At this point I've experienced most of the possible frightening outcomes, and I'm still alive, as is my business. This is why, while I may be intense during the day, when people ask me how I sleep at night, I tell them I sleep like a fucking baby. Detachment doesn't mean I'm trying less hard. It just means that fears and emotions that used to torment and paralyze me no longer have the same power over me. Getting to this point hasn't always been easy; it took me years to really learn to silence my mind. But as you move through your career and your life, you will have to learn that if you're not what you do, then what you do has no business keeping you entertained at night.

When I first started People's Revolution in Los Angeles in the midnineties, it had one employee: me. I did all my own FedExing, answered my own phone, and crafted all my own pitches to the press. I even got my own coffee. Not that this held me back. After the Wasteland's feature in *Vogue*, I set my sights on *People*, which soon ran a huge spread highlighting the store's crocheted shrugs, worn by celebrities like Erykah Badu and Fiona Apple at the time. When I signed the Sunset Marquis Hotel, I was suddenly a fashion and lifestyle publicist making $7,000 a month with virtually no overhead. (*This*, I still believe, is a genius way to do PR.) As People's Revolution grew, I hired an assistant, incorporated my business, took on a partner, rented a cute little house in West Hollywood as my office, and took on even *more* clients to be able to afford all this. But the Mother was right when she said that taking your spirituality to the streets and actually putting it to work is much harder than living in an ashram and meditating all day (or reading tarot cards in the beach, as the case may be). I soon found myself victimized by familiar thought patterns— most persistently fear—despite my newfound spiritual perspective. I had more to lose materially than I'd had in a while, so some fear was inevitable, even productive. But when a prestigious client like Bulgari or Valentino left, as PR clients eventually do, I became convinced that my whole business would collapse. I worried constantly about clients leaving me or staff members quitting. I couldn't shake the notion that *they* were somehow responsible for my success—not me.

My fears got so out of hand that I didn't even need an actual event to trigger them. A single thought would creep uninvited into my mind at the grocery store, at my desk, or even when I was having sex, and suddenly I'd be barreling down this freeway of fear, and it would be packed, with no off-ramps or exit signs. *Something really bad is going to happen to you, you'd better work harder, something really bad is going to happen to you, he's going to fire you, you're going to lose everything, you're going to be all by yourself, you'll be HOMELESS. And by the way, that guy you're dating is cheating on you!* These thoughts would have their way with me, wracking me with self-doubt and paranoia, then leave me by the side of the road, spent. I'd have another three or four days of freedom before they came back again. *You're a faker, you're going to lose everything; you know it's true.*

How did I get to this place? And why was I so attached to the things I had anyway? I called Mikael, my longtime spiritual adviser in India and a prominent member of my tribal council; I'd met Mikael through a friend years earlier and had been consulting with him on matters such as these ever since.* He suggested that I fight my incessant internal chatter: "Your problem is that your name means 'Warrior,' but all you are is a Worrier," he said. "Why don't you drop the 'O' and put in an 'A'?" Once I started thinking of myself as a spiritual warrior, my life started making a lot more sense. I turned to the controversial anthropologist and

* Mikael is the one constant in my life who doesn't live in the United States, work in the fashion business, or want any of my money.

philosopher Carlos Castaneda. He described the warrior in *The Wheel of Time: The Shamans of Mexico, Their Thoughts About Life, Death, and the Universe*:

> We talk to ourselves incessantly about our world. In fact we maintain our world with our internal talk. And whenever we finish talking to ourselves about ourselves and our world, the world is always as it should be. We renew it, we rekindle it with life, we uphold it with our internal talk. Not only that, but we also choose our paths as we talk to ourselves. Thus we repeat the same choices over and over until the day we die, because we keep on repeating the same internal talk over and over until the day we die. A warrior is aware of this and strives to stop his internal talk.

My "internal talk" was not just a nuisance: it was trapping me in repetitive action and paralyzing me into *in*action. I had become a deer in the headlights of my own life. And I wasn't alone: many people spend large portions of their lives in this state. Fear is big business, and companies from Hollywood studios to insurance giants spend millions of dollars a year to keep our freeways of fear packed and our "internal talk" on high volume: *Wow, your child was just admitted to the hospital with a life-threatening illness, too bad you didn't switch to Geico!* Or: *New York City is going to be demolished by a giant tidal wave!* Or: *If you don't buy this product, you'll look wrinkled and old and no man will ever want you!* Our minds—inclined toward repetition, not progress—absorb and play all this back to us in difficult times, parroting society's negative views on women in power, dwelling on past failures, or repeating nasty things our clients have said to us. The mind uses fear throughout our lives as one of many blunt objects with which to clock our soul over the head before gagging it, binding it with black electrical tape, and throwing it out of the driver's seat and into the trunk. This is what sends us off the path of our destiny and onto the packed freeway of fear—or worse, into a traffic circle (and we all know how dangerous those are). For all my supposed spirituality, I had to get out of my own way. I was so caught up in doomsday visions of the future that I'd entirely lost sight of any joy in the present.

So I started to play ball with my fears. "Bring it!" I'd say when seized by that familiar pit in my stomach. Or: "Party on, motherfucker, tell me more." I asked my fear exactly what it had to say to me. *You're going to lose everything and you'll be out on the street.* "Okay," I'd reply. "I can stay with friends." *Well, you can only do that for three days, since they're going to get tired of you.* "All right, well, then, I can go to Virginia and stay with my parents. And I'll totally lose my mind there, but I'll only be there for six months, because in six months I will have thought of something that will get me back on my feet. Or, plan B, if I go out of business, I'll move to southern India, where I'll teach in a school and have no money to ever travel back to the U.S." I followed my fears to their worst possible conclusions, becoming penniless and alone (these are most people's worst fears), and what I realized each time was that no matter what happened, I was going to be *fine*. I remembered that family and tribe members are key, but also that ultimately I have everything I need to survive inside of me.

There are a million other yogic tricks a warrior can use to quiet his or her mind and banish it to the backseat (or better yet, the trunk). Some people suggest watching your fears like a movie in your head until you become desensitized to them. I also like writing them down over and over again, hundreds of times—*I'm going to lose everything, I'm going to lose everything, I'm going to lose everything, I'm going to lose everything*—until the words lose their power. Then I can burn the paper in the kitchen sink and literally watch them turn to smoke. (If you're really feeling adventurous, you could try this in your backyard or in one of those holy places I told you to visit!) There is also the garden metaphor: your negative thoughts are weeds strangling the progress of your soul; you must find a way to kill them. Killing the weeds won't keep them from growing back, but it's like waxing: eventually, if you keep waxing, your hair growth just becomes less and less.

The problem with "internal talk" is that it masquerades as intuition. Sometimes your fears really are conveying a message from your inner voice, whether it's telling you to work harder or pointing out that you're dating a domineering asshole who will never change. This is why a warrior needs a highly developed sense of discernment. Fear of losing everything becomes less irrational in a worldwide recession, after all. My company had been on a huge streak when the economy began its long plunge in 2008, and suddenly certain clients couldn't pay their bills and I found myself having to be their psychotherapist in addition to their accountant and publicist. I had thoughts like, *Did I really work my ass off to build this business for the last twelve years only to have it all come crashing down on top of me?* I was seriously considering closing my Paris office and wondering whom I'd have to sue for payment. Rather than banish my fear, or think *That's preposterous, that'll never happen to me, I'm protected by the Goddess,* I knew it made sense to ask, *Am I being wasteful somewhere? Are my results less than they have been? How do I receive my clients when they call me? How do I decrease my overhead and increase my revenue?* I like to think of fear as a messenger that doesn't always make sense: you have to figure out who sent fear before you can dismiss it outright.

I learned to do this in the long, arduous days after my drug detox, when I'd moved out of the run-down Beverly Laurel Motel and into a tiny apartment on Spaulding, where I formed a habit of scrounging together sixty-eight cents every afternoon to run down the street to the gas station to buy a doughnut. I followed this routine like clockwork. Four o'clock would roll around, and I *had* to have a doughnut. After all, I was off other substances, and I really loved these doughnuts. One day John asked me why I was always running out for a doughnut. "Close your eyes and ask yourself what would happen if you did not get that doughnut," he said. "I really need a doughnut," I said. I knew by that time that spirituality is often about doing away with things we've become attached to, and frankly, I wasn't in the mood. Still, I closed my eyes and asked myself what would happen if I didn't go out for a doughnut. That's when a thunderous voice inside me shrieked, *"You will die!!!"* "Well, then," said John, satisfied, "do you really think that is the voice of God?" I've used this so-called doughnut barometer over the years in moments when I am gripped by worries over anything from my daughter's safety to my ability to make my payroll. If you ask yourself often enough, *Is this the voice of God?* the answer usually becomes obvious. A voice telling you that you suck, that you're not important, that you're heading toward impending doom of some kind or another, is probably not the voice of your soul, or the Divine, or the Goddess. But if there *is* an important message to be found in your thought, you must take positive action immediately in order to glean it. For me, during the recession, that meant calling my clients more often to check in, cutting costs, more actively managing certain accounts, and laying off staff members who weren't pulling their weight. Once you've acted positively on a legitimate fear to the best of your ability, then, if it persists, it's time to banish that fear to the backseat too.

If you allow fear to live inside of you after you've already put it to any possible good use—if you allow your mind, instead of your soul, to drive your car—you risk more than just finding yourself on a hamster wheel. You also increase the possibility that you'll manifest that fear and negative thinking outwardly. One of my best friends—a totally hot, sexy woman and one of the coolest women I've ever met—once fell madly in love with an actor twenty-five years younger than she was. The age difference gave her pause, but she decided to marry him anyway. They were very happy together, except for one thing: she was terrified on a daily basis that he was going to leave her for a younger woman. *Every. Day.* She'd say things like, "Oh my God, he's in an acting class, those girls are so pretty, I feel so old, oh my God!" Soon enough she got pregnant, at which point her fears only intensified: "Oh my God, I'm so fat, he's going to leave me, *Oh. My. God!*" What do you think happened? After four years of marriage, her husband came home one day and said, "I'm leaving you." He left her for someone his own age. I don't think he would have left her had that not already been her reality. Thoughts have power. Fear of being left was so much a part of her world and her thinking that she manifested her own divorce.

I believe that the universe constantly rearranges itself to support your idea of reality. If you're always thinking, *Life sucks, and I suck*, you're definitely going to see a lot of dismal shit out there. On the other hand, if your idea of reality is that you're a privileged, elegant human being and every day you think, *I am a privileged, elegant human being, I am a privileged, elegant human being*, then eventually you will become a privileged and elegant human being. It may take five minutes or it may take five years, but that will become your experience of yourself.

Fighting the tyranny of your mind and freeing yourself to enjoy the journey, stumbles and all, is a lifelong process. There will be plenty of days in your life and career when you feel like you literally do not have air left in your lungs. I haven't exactly cured myself of fear and doubt either. Sometimes, while sitting in my office late at night, I'll feel it welling up inside of me and have to say, *"Oh my God, are you still there? How much longer are we going to be in this relationship?"*

In the summer of 2002, with New York still reeling from the job losses and concentrated regional despair of September 11, 2001, the fashion industry held several town hall meetings to discuss how to handle Fashion Week, which would fall on the one-year anniversary of 9/11 (and which had been in progress during the attacks). We wondered: Where is the rule book for this? Are we allowed to do something so frivolous and shallow as a fashion show on the first anniversary of such a tragedy, with so many people to be honored and so many families' feelings to be respected? How will there ever be a place again for something like Fashion Week? As concern among my colleagues grew, I knew *I* didn't want to live in fear and try to be less than celebratory so that everyone could feel okay on a day that I thought should be a celebration of the strength of a people and our ability to *not* be held back by fear. I also thought Fashion Week was a great way to bring beauty back into the world. So while my competitors backed off the fashion show time slots at the Bryant Park tents on September 11, 2002, I made a deal with IMG—the company that produces Fashion Week—to take all three tents for my clients and produce an arduous load of six shows on the same day, among them Asfour, Jeremy Scott, Alexandre Herchcovitz, and Rachel Comey. I was able to wrangle good financial deals for these clients, who were thrilled.

However, even though I haven't exactly made a career for myself by playing it safe, some industry friends were scared for me. They thought my clients would be overshadowed by media attention to the anniversary, and they worried about how the press would react to fashion shows being held on such a day. I had plenty of moments when I wondered what I'd gotten myself into (and whether anyone would come to the shows), but ultimately my fears were mere shadows of what they might have been ten years earlier. The Fashion Week experience that year was kind of like giving birth: I was going to have this baby, and it was going to be fine. That day, as I dashed furiously between tents, presiding over backstage areas in rehearsal while catching snippets of my clients' actual shows on the television monitors set up outside in the park for passersby, I also felt a great sigh of relief from my colleagues. Many had seen their shows canceled the year before, after all, and their businesses had been devastated in the last year. The industry was grateful that business was going on as usual, and I was proud to be a part of that.

We've already established that life is going to kick you in your ass sometimes and that there's no way to avoid that, but if you get up and keep doing what you do, giving your best self each time, you eventually achieve not only success but that great psychic coup of detachment. After years of worrying that banks would close me down, that clients wouldn't pay me, or that I'd get sued for missing articles of clothing that weren't returned to me by editors, I now employ four lawyers and do business through airtight contracts, and when I'm served with court papers, my response is more like: "Oh, hi, how are you?" The fashion industry is excellent yoga for a naturally fearful person like me in part because its fast-paced, apocalyptic energy requires that you feel and act, not think. In fact, for years I'd call Mikael with a problem and say, "What do you think about that?" and he would reply, "I do not think. I feel." There are some things that the Goddess just takes away from us—my addiction, for example—and others that we're supposed to work through step by step in this lifetime so that we can have the power of victory over them. Often you can't achieve this victory without experiencing pain until you have no emotional, physical, or psychic response to it anymore.

Take my old fear of losing my business when a client fired me. A few years ago, a fashion designer client asked me to meet him to discuss his upcoming show. He wanted to review the collection and hear all my ideas about what he should do for the next six months. At the end of our meeting, having gotten the whole thing on tape, he fired me. It was frustrating to give all this freshness and good intent to the relationship with the understanding that it was a continuing collaboration, and then to have my ideas basically stolen. But I didn't flinch. His words didn't penetrate me or send me careening off-course. I'd already spent years asking myself whether I was a good publicist and a hard worker and a valid person, and I knew the answers to those questions. I just told him he was a disgusting human being and that any time I had the opportunity to share that with other people in the industry, it would be my pleasure.

In an industry like fashion, people always behave badly all around you, but if you resolve to become a spiritual warrior, you learn to laugh and laugh, knowing that other people don't define you and that ultimately their behavior is just helping you work out your own shit. For a publicist, being fired can be its very own yoga! I personally have been practicing it for years, and I can now say I'm an expert.

Several years ago, I represented Brad Korzen, a now-prominent hotelier best known for the design-y Viceroy Hotels. We launched his first signature property, the Avalon in Beverly Hills, we helped christen it a fashion-crowd hangout, and we even helped transform his girlfriend (now his wife), Kelly Wearstler, from *Playboy* pet to *Vogue*-sanctioned interior designer. But one

Monday morning not long before Brad was to open the Viceroy in Santa Monica, he called me up and said, "Did you know more people kill themselves on Monday than any other day of the year?" I admitted that this was news to me. "Listen," he continued, "I just want to tell you that you're a really great publicist, but you're the only publicist I've ever had, and I thought it would be good to change the energy up a bit before the Viceroy opens. But I also want to tell you that if I'm not happy, I'll come back to you, and I hope that we can remain friends." Ouch. I was tempted to allow the situation to drag me into familiar thought patterns: *What's wrong with me? Am I a bad publicist? Is my business going to tank? Maybe I need to be smarter, maybe I need to work harder, maybe I need to part my hair differently, maybe I need to wear more makeup, maybe I need to wear* less *makeup, maybe I need to be clearer in my speech? Is my business going to tank?* But I knew that People's Revolution had done an excellent job for Brad and that he'd been written up all over the world. I had also already been fired enough times to know that Brad wouldn't make or break me. Instead of collapsing into sobs, as I might have at twenty-four, I picked up my scepter. "Okay," I told Brad. "But let me tell *you* something. I feel like I've been married to you for seventeen years and you just told me you want to go out and fuck the tennis coach. Fine, go fuck the tennis coach, but don't come back to my house afterwards."

SIX

CHECK YOUR PRECONCEIVED NOTIONS AT THE DOOR

Not even the slickest
wordsmith or spinning
spin master can describe
the delight and dedication
which is motherhood. This
is a secret society which
words cannot touch, but
the heart holds dear.

—Kelly Cutrone

For women, life is set up like a video game. It starts out in childhood with the Disney princesses, followed by the need to become the prettiest girl, the pop star, or the model, and then, in high school, we're told that it's time to become the thinnest girl, then to become successful, find a guy, convince him to move in with us, get married, have a baby, and live happily ever after! (Hell, *yeah*!) We're constantly moving from level to level, trying to collect the promised prizes, without stopping to think about the order *we* want these things to come in, or whether we even really want them at all. From *Cinderella* right on up to *He's Just Not That into You*, we're inundated with programming that influences how and when we think we should experience various life steps and that makes it devastating when we find ourselves in another position altogether. Many of us grew up with our mothers literally serenading us with the words: *First comes love, then comes marriage, then comes a baby in a baby carriage.* Yes, our own mothers! The Life-bringers themselves are in on this conspiracy.

The unavoidable truth is that in the real world things don't always come in the order we're taught to expect them. A lot of women ask me, "How do you have it all?" I tell them that it's not actually that hard to have it all; you just can't always have it all in the same proportion or at the same time. Sometimes your career is winning, sometimes it's your peace of mind, sometimes it's your faith, sometimes it's motherhood, and occasionally, if you're lucky, it's your love life. I didn't set out to become a single mother, but I was not totally surprised when I became one at thirty-five—even though I'd been married twice by then. Long-term relationships are difficult for me. I also have a hard time biting my tongue. If my partner's flirting with a waitress at a diner, I'm going to want to go at it on that topic right then and there, whereas people who live together peacefully are probably able to let some things pass. I was forced to accept at a certain point that I was likely to end up on my own. But as I do with most glorious, challenging, and worthwhile tasks, I not only made the best of my single, unplanned mother-hood but *excelled* at it. And I learned that when things happen out of order in your life, you can choose to take them not as blows but as blessings in disguise.

I found out I was pregnant with my daughter Ava at 11:30 p.m. on September 10, 2001, smack in the middle of New York Fashion Week. I was making my way back to my SoHo loft after a long day of producing runway shows and had stopped at a pharmacy, where I bought a box of Honey Nut Cheerios (something I had a strange new passion for), paper towels, laundry detergent, and a pregnancy test. To be honest, I don't even remember purchasing the test, but when I got home, there it was in my bag. I figured that, like the other tests I'd taken over the years, this one would turn out negative, a result I'd always greeted with a burst of relief and a tinge of hidden sadness. But no, not this night. I was soon staring at two pink bars. And, well, I was delighted!

It wasn't exactly the best timing. If someone had told me I'd be separating from my second husband, breaking up with my original partner in People's Revolution, moving from Los Angeles back to New York to run a growing bicoastal company, and draining my savings account to pay a team of lawyers to oversee these changes—all while pregnant by a man who was not my husband but rather an incredibly sophisticated and sexy Italian nine years my junior who I'd met in Paris while producing my first couture show—even *I* would have said they were crazy. I'd finally moved into my spacious new home and office on Grand Street just in time to see my world—and *the* world—utterly change.

I remember running upstairs before I went to bed that night to grab *Savitri*, an epic tome by Sri Aurobindo, the Indian philosopher who was the Mother's spiritual partner. I closed my eyes as I flipped through the pages, thinking, *Is this something I'm meant to do now? Is this the right time? Mother, please tell me: what is this about?* It was my way of asking for a sign that I could handle motherhood on top of a life that was already careening again toward insanity—even if much less destructively than the first time around in my early twenties. My finger landed on a paragraph that talked about new children coming down the amber stairs from the Divine into this world. It read:

I saw the Omnipotent's flaming pioneers
Over the heavenly verge which turns towards life
Come crowding down the amber stairs of birth;
Forerunners of a divine multitude,
Out of the paths of the morning star they came
Into the little room of mortal life.
I saw them cross the twilight of an age,
The sun-eyed children of a marvellous dawn.

I felt like the Goddess was talking to me through the pages of this book, telling me that my unborn daughter was one of "the Omnipotent's flaming pioneers." I'd opened to the only page of the book's 956 pages that even mentioned children. Taking the passage as a clear sign that my pregnancy was indeed meant to be, I called my daughter's father, Ilario. We'd been dating for only two months, but we were in love, and he was very excited to hear the news. Next I called my friend Myra, a fifty-two-year-old power-girl publicist who had never had children. "Kelly," she said, "this is a blessing. We are going to have *so much fun!*"

My parents were a different story. "I know you're in love with Romeo or whatever his name is, but being a mother and being in love are two different things," cautioned my father when I called to share the news. "I *know* you, and this relationship might not last, so you need to ask yourself, do you want to be a mother or do you just want to be a family? Because those are often two different things." He ended our conversation with a vote of confidence in me. "If you were eighteen years old, we'd be having a different conversation," he said. "But you're thirty-five, and if anyone can do this, Kel, it's you." It was good advice, especially coming from a man who had once threatened the life of my prom date.

My mom, who had already taken in several of my dogs, was less supportive. She wanted to make sure I was in a position to actually *watch* this child. At that point I became very upset with her for even raising such a question and told her that if she continued to speak like that she'd never meet her grandchild. I had a lot of unknowns in my life, but I never doubted for one minute that I'd be a good mother. I reminded my mom that I'd been raising young women in my office for years, not to mention devotedly taking care of my clients, and that the only reason I'd shipped my dog off to her anyway was that I was living on Christopher Street at the time and the poor beast happened to be terrified of drag queens. In other words: *how dare she?*

My euphoria was short-lived. The next morning my phone rang. It was Ilario, calling from Paris to tell me he'd just watched a plane crash into one of the World Trade Center towers on TV. I looked out my window and saw the second plane hit, and then the two towers were suddenly engulfed in flames, just blocks from my apartment. This was the moment I became a mother. I ran to the back of my loft, still cluttered with boxes, and began sweetly consoling Ava in my womb. "Do not worry," I told her. "We are going to be just *fine*, baby, just fine."

Weeks passed, and as my father had stopped short of predicting, Ilario and I split up—distance and hormones were not on our side—leaving me single, well on my way to gaining a whopping seventy pounds, and struggling to run a business in a wounded, reeling city that seemed eerily abandoned. I finally had to acknowledge that the modern, very empowered, very *difficult* version of motherhood I was about to undertake would be nothing like the one I'd always envisioned. I had been raised to think that I'd be married at the birth of my child, that a man would be present in the delivery room, and that he would put a cold compress on my forehead and give me ice pops and buy me a birth gift. Instead, I had a stick-thin fashion editor and a lesbian couple vying to see me through to the delivery room. As much as I appreciated their can-do, girl-power camaraderie, I was scared to death. This was not the VIP list at a nightclub; it was the birth of my child, and when it came down to it, I was alone.

I tried to console myself with thoughts like, *How much harder can this be than having a dog?* At the time I had a beloved Boston terrier named Japa. Unfortunately, about a month into my pregnancy, she was eaten by coyotes in L.A., where I'd sent her to stay with my soon-to-be ex-husband while I was busy with Fashion Week. When I heard the news of her death, I began crying hysterically in my office. It sounded like whales mating. All heads in the office turned in my direction as the troops froze in fear: *Leader having breakdown! Leader having breakdown!* I couldn't shake the possible symbolism here. Eaten by coyotes! What did it mean? Was this what became of sentient beings for whom I was responsible? I immediately called Mikael, who tried to console me by explaining that Japa was a guardian and a protector, that her work here was done, and that her death had nothing to do with my pregnancy. That still didn't change the fact that I was single, emotional, and pregnant and my dog was dead.

Luckily, I had little time to sit around thinking, *What's going to happen to me?* I was gaining weight the way only a Mediterranean village girl could, which distracted me from the larger, more terrifying issues at hand and helped me focus on several urban single power-girl pregnancy challenges. First, I could *not* wear maternity clothes—ugh, yuck, no way, no thanks, never! Pea in the Pod made me want to kill myself. What were these fabrics? *Floral prints?* I was sure I'd rather clean toilets than be seen in them. And as for those little tie-back tunics infesting downtown Manhattan's paltry selection of maternity boutiques: maybe useful as a beach umbrella in Tunisia, darling, but they certainly weren't meant to be worn. After all, I was no longer a music publicist—I was in fashion. It was bad enough that I had to carry my groceries in the middle of winter by myself—I could not possibly do it in these outfits. Their bland, vaguely submissive frilliness threatened to drain all of my hard-won strength and ball-busting, soon-to-be single mom courage. In a moment of deep sartorial despair I called a friend at *Vogue* magazine. "What am I going to do?" I complained. "I cannot be seen in these clothes. They'll put me out of business *and* into a mental hospital!" She told me to go to a Hare Krishna temple—this was what she'd done during her pregnancy—to buy a series of Indian Punjabi outfits in muted tones. She warned me that black might not be available.

I have to say, the Krishnas make a lovely vegetarian lunch, and their oversized pure cotton clothes were an oasis in a depressing polyester pregnancy-wear slum.

Burgeoning curves accommodated, I began fretting that I'd

be fired by some of my image-conscious clients for getting fat. (This was long before Nicole Richie and Angelina Jolie started on procreative tears and baby bumps became a hot accessory in *Us Weekly*.) I managed to keep my condition a secret from clients and professional acquaintances for just two months, at which point the legendary designer Paco Rabanne outed me during Paris Fashion Week after I produced his runway show. "Kell-eee, why didn't you tell us you were pregnant?" he screamed. We were eating lunch with a bunch of editors and industry friends at the Costes, the trendy fashion hotel for rich attention-seekers (and certainly one of the last places on earth I'd want to have my secret revealed at deafening volume). Paco, who considers himself something of a psychic, informed the group with certainty that it would be a girl. There were screams of *"What?"* as everyone looked to me for confirmation, which I provided with a tentative nod.

Luckily, Paco didn't fire me; those fears, at least, were unfounded. But I still had others to address, such as: could I really go alone to birthing classes? I didn't think I could stomach the idea of watching yuppie couples *Ooooo* and *Ahhhh* together on yoga mats while I sat huffing and puffing alone. I don't even like group sports. Besides, girls of fifteen and sixteen in some parts of the world just walk into rice fields and pop out babies all on their own. I was thirty-five years old, a woman of the world; surely I could manage this. I decided to skip the birthing classes.

Instead, I turned to a doula, the hottest new concept in childbirthing. I met Amy Brown, a ripped, no-nonsense, very New York birth coach who looked like Linda Hamilton in *Terminator*, through my well-connected gynecologist, Dr. Moritz. Amy's role would be to coach me, to serve as an advocate on my behalf at the hospital, and to prevent me from being overmedicated or—worse in her mind—getting an epidural. She was a cross between a best friend, a mom, an action hero, and a lawyer, and she was definitely more competent than a husband would have been at running my birth experience.

At our first interview, she asked me who my pregnancy role model was. Sad but true, I couldn't think of one woman I looked up to in that way. I'd never been involved in anyone's birth. I didn't know anything *about* birth. The only thing that came to mind was yet another beloved former pet, Cinder, who, after being impregnated by her brother Miles—my other dog at the time—popped out eight puppies on my favorite Jean-Paul Gaultier coat. The thing I loved about Cinder was that, despite getting bigger by the day and eating more than her share (just like me!), she was completely oblivious to the fact that she was pregnant and went on with her life as usual. For dogs, pregnancy is a normal state.

I told Amy that my role model for birth was my dog Cinder. Then she asked me, "How do you envision your birth?" and I told her that I thought I'd be alone in the middle of the night. She asked me if I had any fears about that. "I just don't want any strangers to see me naked," I said.

This especially applied to hot, younger strangers who happened to be models, it turned out. During Fashion Week in February, I was enlisted to produce my first men's show, J. Lindeberg. When I was incredibly large, alone, and five months pregnant, it was just my luck to be subjected to a parade of the world's most beautiful men. I tried to direct them to a bathroom to change, but most would strip down to their underwear right in front of me, as models tend to do. I was sure the Goddess was trying to kill me. The feeling only intensified one day when a young Italian model named Stefano arrived at my office limping: his bicycle had been hit by a cab. I asked him if he was okay, and I calmed him down. But when he rode his bicycle back to my office the next day bearing biscotti (he owned a biscotti company with his brother—I mean, *please*) and admitted to a crush on me, I freaked out. I had a conservative Betty Crocker streak that recoiled at the thought of kissing a man while pregnant with another man's child. But how do you tell a smolderingly hot Italian model fifteen years your junior who is miraculously oblivious to your rotund figure that you're just not interested? Poor Stefano continued to send biscotti for the next several months anyway, but from then on my only suitors were the very forward Haitian bike messengers who showed up at my office every day to pick up or return clothes for photo shoots.

So I embarked on a love affair with Swedish Fish. I would walk down the street working my way through bags and bags of them; with no coffee, cigarettes, or sex, I needed *something*. One day, as I chomped mindlessly, a little voice spoke to me with perfect clarity: "Hi, my name's Ava. It means free like a bird." I went back to my office and looked it up, and indeed, that's what it meant. I'd been mulling names for months, weighing classics like Camilla with my personal favorite, Indira (a possibility squashed by Mikael, who insisted that I could not name my daughter after someone assassinated in my lifetime). I hired women all the time, so I was aware of how a name could set a person up in life. I wanted my daughter to share my last name, Cutrone, but it was also important that the name go well with Ilario's last name, in case she ever wanted to hyphenate. And now it was settled: Ava, perfect on all counts. My daughter was directing her own destiny already.

Two weeks before my due date, at around midnight, I was listening on the phone as my fashion editor friend blabbered about various ill-fated love interests—something so out of the realm of possibility for me at that point that it was difficult to endure that kind of talk—when she asked if I thought I was going to have the baby soon. "I wish I'd go into labor right now!" I exclaimed. No sooner did the words leave my mouth than *pop*—water came pouring out of me. *Oh my God*, I thought. *I've just wished my own labor.*

"Do not move," said my friend breathlessly. "I am on my way!" Oh, *great*. Despite her good intentions, she was high-strung and literally the last person I wanted to see in the delivery room. In fact, her offer of assistance with the birth was what had prompted me to hire Amy in the first place. I called up my assistant to get my team on the phone. "Cancel all my meetings for the week!" I roared. "I'm having a baby!"

Speedy Gonzales arrived at my door and informed me there was a cab waiting downstairs. "No way am I going in a taxi—call a car service!" I cried. I mindlessly grabbed a pair of jeans, thinking I could wear them home from the hospital. *Ha!* I'd be stuck in my shapeless punjabis for months to come.

By that time my pelvis was opening like a pyramid door.

Eeeeeeeeeeeeeeeee, it creaked, as if a secret code were causing it to slowly and painfully rip apart (this was an understatement). By the time Amy arrived, I was vomiting and had taken to swinging my arms to and fro like an ape to distract myself from the pain and she was looking like the best $3,000 I'd ever spent. Surely she could suppress my excitable fashion editor friend, who had turned herself out for my labor in a red turtleneck in the middle of May and was now repeating, like a parrot: "We've got to get out of here! We've got to get out of here!"

We made our way downstairs to pile into the car, a smashing trio. Our driver was a very young Sikh who seemed a bit embarrassed by the howling of these three witches of the night. "Sixty-nine blocks straight up the West Side Highway to St. Luke's!" Amy cried. But at Thirty-second Street, I told the driver to pull over because I had to pee. "Do *not* listen to her!" Amy countered. "She's fully dilated, we need to get her to the hospital!"

"Pull the fuck over or I will fucking jump out of this car!" I screeched. The driver obeyed, startled. I threw off my punjabi pants and was soon naked from the waist down, squatting on the side of the West Side Highway, attempting to pee. "Nothing is coming out," I called in the direction of the car. Amy replied that it was the pressure of the baby and ordered me to get back in. Meanwhile, trucks beeped and passengers cheered as my worst fears about strangers seeing me naked were realized a hundred times over before I even got to the hospital.

I jumped back into the car, situating myself backward on my knees, staring out at the lights of the city through the rear window. My body felt like a pinball machine, every light ignited with pain, blinking and throbbing. I could sense that it knew what to do, and the baby knew what to do, but my mind was still screeching, *Get me out of here!* I fired off a desperate eleventh-hour prayer to the Goddess, offering to remain in a state of pregnancy for the rest of my life if I could just skip what was about to happen.

We stampeded into St. Luke's, Amy massaging my back, me screaming at the frightened nurses: *"I want drugs! I want drugs! I want drugs!"* I sensed them whispering about me, and in short order they were trying to interfere with the beatific and very trendy water birth I'd hoped for. At this point two of my three longtime birth fantasies had already been slashed—the one involving living in Venice while pregnant and delivering at the American Hospital there, and the one involving, you know, a *man*—and I wasn't about to give this last one up that easily.

"She is over thirty-five, we need to get her on a fetal heart monitor," one nurse directed. *"I want a water birth!"* I bellowed. "Well, even if you get in the water, you need to get out of the tub and have your baby on a bed for insurance reasons in New York State," replied another nurse. *"Get the fuck out of here, I do not ever want to speak to or see any of you ever again!"* I screamed, and they left. Finally the bossy nurses had met their match.

Eventually Dr. Moritz appeared. "Kelly Cutrone, of all the fashion girls who are having a natural childbirth in New York City this morning," he said with a laugh. He'd been hearing from me regularly for at least a month. "Moritz!" I'd shriek from my office. "I can't take this anymore! I haven't seen my feet in months, I can't zip my boots, and I'm wearing Amish clogs!"

He'd offered to schedule a C-section, of course, explaining that this was what women like me (translation: nightmare, rich) were doing now, for astrological or work reasons. But my conservative Betty Crocker streak had intervened yet again, prompting me to go natural. Now here I was pleading for pharmaceutical relief. "I want some drugs!" I cried. "Anything!"

He pointed to his left shoulder. "Put your leg up here, baby, and push, and I'll give you something afterward." I fell in love with Dr. Moritz in that moment. He was part care bear, part knight in shining armor, and he more than made up for any masculinity lacking in my birth equation. I forgot all about my water birth and began to push. There is not one writer in the world who can accurately describe the feeling of giving birth (or getting tattooed, for that matter), so I won't waste your time. Suffice it to say that before long there was Ava: head, shoulders, *swoosh*, spilling out of me. It was less *Born Free* than *Species*. Amy held my hand and cheered me on while the fashion editor cowered in the corner, probably in awe of my vagina, which had not been waxed in months.

Since everything I knew about childbirth had been gleaned from birthing shows on TLC, I was convinced I would cry my eyes out when I first saw Ava. Instead, when she emerged, I was speechless for the first time that day. (Surely the nurses were grateful.) They immediately put her on my chest. She wasn't even crying, and she was already cool. Who was this little being, and how did she come through me like that? Oh my God, she wants to breast-feed already? And now I have to deliver something called the placenta? The *what*? Maybe they'd covered this in the birthing classes I skipped, but birthing one's placenta can only be compared to putting a flaming drink from Trader Vic's onto your vagina after a marathon night of banging a football player. When it was over, the nurses showed it to me. It was bigger than a Frisbee and full of membranes and blood. "Would you like to take this home with you?" they inquired. "What planet are you *living* on?" I replied.

A mere twelve hours after this ordeal, the nurses told me I was free to go home. "Are you kidding me?" I protested. "I'm going nowhere!" I had heard that you could order gourmet food delivery in New York hospitals, and it was true: you could. (I recommend giving birth in New York City for this reason alone.) My mother arrived that night, and we holed up in the hospital for the two full days allowed by my insurance, ordering in elaborate meals. It was only Wednesday, after all, and I had no interest in decamping to my home/office until my employees were gone for the weekend.

My full-floor SoHo loft housed People's Revolution in the front and my two-room apartment in the back. (People's Revolution would later expand to fill three floors, and my own apartment one floor.) I had pledged to Amy to continue breast-feeding once I left the hospital, even though it felt like rolling your nipples in broken glass while someone shoots hot oil through every vein of your breast. This confused my mother, who had grown up in a middle-class household in the 1950s and was of the opinion that breast-feeding was for dirty hippies and "Third World people." "I guess that's what you kids are doing these days," she'd say incredulously, shaking her head. By the third day I was a walking zombie. I tried to channel my younger days as a groovy "It" girl who regularly stayed out until four or five a.m. in nightclubs. Why did I now find these hours to be such an inconvenience?

My mother and I had other generational differences on the subject of my breasts. When Ava was four days old, we took her out to dinner in Little Italy, where I proceeded to nurse at the table. My mother was mortified. I patiently explained to her that this was not a porn movie; I was feeding my child. Nonetheless, in insisting that I cover up, she became one of the many women who would balk in knee-jerk fashion at the sight of my breasts being used for their natural purpose. Once she left town, I bared my boobs all over the world—beside catwalks from New York to Paris and in a meeting with twelve Greek shipping magnates who wanted to talk to me about their image. My tits were like the SoHo welcoming committee.

Most of the time, though, I was genuinely relieved to have my mother's company during Ava's first days. I remember looking over at her, exhausted after two days of no sleep, and saying: "I'm so sorry for anything I've ever said or done to you." I suddenly had this deep understanding of what a mother does for a child. It's as if, during labor, Mother Nature implants a computer chip in your brain that makes you want to love this person you don't even know, so that after three days of nonstop breastfeeding, when you leave the baby with your mom and venture out for a quick slice of pizza, there's suddenly this voice in your head shrieking, "You need to go back to the baby *right now!*" And yet you look at your child and you just know from the beginning that she's going to break your heart. You just know it. You know she's going to steal your credit card and your cell phone and lie to you and call you a bitch because she has a crush on some guy you don't like. But you love her and *want* for her anyway, and it's the most beautiful, selfless love; you instinctively know you'd do anything for her, regardless of what she does to you. My mother stayed four days after Ava's birth before returning to my sick father, and when she left I cried like a baby. "I can't believe you're leaving me here alone!" I wailed at the front door.

I soon had plenty of people volunteering to come over and help, but to my great relief, I found that it's a natural thing to be with your child. People in the West make it into such a big thing, this feat that's going to take twenty-five around-the-clock helpers. But my nanny didn't start until Ava was several weeks old, and in that time my daughter and I developed a rhythm we've maintained to this day. We're in sync. We're separate, but she feels almost like a continuation of me. We still sleep in the same bed, like wolves. We got so comfortable together that after two weeks I realized I had to get off the couch or I was going to become addicted to *Judge Judy*. That's a bad sign, when the highlight in your life is *Judge Judy*. I remember sitting crumpled in a naked heap on the floor one day, breast-feeding Ava, staring down at my ravaged body with its uncut toenails and downward-pointing breasts, and thinking, *I need a pedicure and a wax*.

I began bringing Ava to the office and breast-feeding her in staff meetings. It was an amazing time during which I discovered some of the benefits of single motherhood. You're not sharing your time, or your decisions, with anyone else. You're not trying to put your child to bed to have sex with your husband, and you're not arguing about the child's religion. (I have friends who are married and can't agree on anything.) Of course, there were also experiences I missed out on, like being intimate with someone in the sixth month of my pregnancy and sharing my excitement with my husband over my breast milk letting down. But to be alone with a child and pick out her name and decide when she's going to go to sleep and where she's going to sleep—there was something exciting about the autonomy of these choices. It proved my theory that when life deals you blows, there are blessings to be found in them if you look hard enough.

As Ava grew and reached certain milestones, I would still have to face brutal reminders of how alone I was. For example, when I was looking for a preschool—an overwhelming task for any parent in Manhattan, but especially a single one—I didn't have a partner I could look to and say, "Can you believe we're doing this? She's eighteen months old already, oh my God!" Instead, I toiled alone, answering application questions like "What is your role in your child's homework?" (She was not even two at the time.) "Ava is a self-starter with an excellent attention span," I'd write. Or: "I'm particularly impressed by the Quaker focus on consensus building and contemplative reflection at your school." During the week of admissions interviews, my lip was literally quivering. I'd had a twitching eyelid before, and I'd had hives and plenty of upset stomachs, but never anything like this—*this* was a whole new level of stress.

It was New York Fashion Week yet again, of course (life in Manhattan can sometimes seem like one continuous Fashion Week), and the dry-erase boards in my office were covered with lists of fashion shows my company was producing and lists of the schools Ava had applied to, reminding us all of deadlines and interview dates. I would stumble out of my Lincoln town car at these interviews, hair totally unkempt, knowing I had just forty-five minutes to make a good impression on some former academic geek of an admissions officer who had probably been waiting his or her whole life to reject cool downtown parents, and then I'd jet back to Bryant Park to put on a runway show. Perhaps this torturous process was why I was excited to hear soon after about a great preschool called the Children's Aid Society, which had an enlightened first-come-first-serve policy and didn't require sign-up until December. Of course, in Manhattan first-come-first-serve really means: "You must wait in line all night. Outside." So I rented an SUV and plotted to park it illegally on the sidewalk for heat, safety, and shelter. (It was December, after all.) How quickly my life had changed: once a fearless creature of the night, pushing my way into packed after-hours nightclubs, I was now terrified to be out on the street alone at three in the morning without the sanctuary of a black SUV.

Luckily, I received a phone call from a client who was genuinely scared that I'd be waiting outside alone in New York to get my daughter into preschool; he told me he had hired a security guard to protect me. It was one of the most touching things a client has ever done for me. As I drove up to the school in my SUV, bracing for my all-nighter, there he was, my security detail, six-foot-four and African-American and loaded up with Freihofer's and Entenmann's to hold us over. We were second in line: the first was a law student who'd been paid by an NYU professor to be

EVERYTHING GOOD HAPPENS AFTER THIRTY

People think their twenties are this really great time because that's when they're hot, but the truth is that we don't even become women, I believe, until we're thirty. I specifically remember being married to my second husband about two weeks after my thirtieth birthday and starting to cry hysterically out of the blue. He asked me if something bad happened at work that day. "No," I told him. "I feel like I'm becoming a woman." And I was: later I would learn that I was experiencing my astrological coming-of-age. Astrologers believe that we don't become adults until our first Saturn returns, which happens between ages twenty-seven and thirty.

The twenties are a time to figure out where you came from and where you're going, and if you're lucky, you're getting closer to these answers by the time you're thirty. You've probably already done everything embarrassing in your twenties, from drugs and binge-drinking to paranoid stalker girlfriend behaviors. Let's face it, the humiliation of getting a locksmith to help you break into your ex-boyfriend's house because you think he's cheating on you even though you're not dating anymore can have a lasting deterrent effect on a person's psyche. Here are ten other things to look forward to after you turn thirty:

[1] Salary increases: If you've followed everything I've told you to do in this book, you'll be making some beaucoup dollars by thirty.

a placeholder. A series of dads eventually lined up behind us—unsurprisingly, there were no other moms—and soon the men were all vying to hang out in my SUV to warm up. I may have been the only parent Ava had at that point, but clearly she was at no disadvantage; $18,000 later, my fears about my ability to over-

[2] After having gone through a plethora of designers for clothing, it's time to step it up a notch and charge headlong into the land of overpriced luxury accessories, where I hope you'll encounter some of the same landmarks I did: Globe-trotter, Asprey, Louboutin, Vuitton, Bulgari, Hermes, Roger Vivier.

[3] A baby. If you want one.

[4] The desire and the emotional wherewithal to date three men at the same time without remorse.

[5] Vacations outside the USA *sans* youth hostel.

[6] Self-control. This is the time when we ride the lion; the lion does not ride us. Like Durga, we sit on top of it and enjoy the ride.

[7] Property ownership, or maybe just your own apartment.

[8] The ability to buy your own muscle car, if you want one.

[9] Decrease in overall paranoia and hysteria, which leads to . . .

[10] Better sex. Definitely better sex. (By this I mean the slow fade of the missionary position and a mind-blowing new cornucopia of sex toys and experiences.)

see her education subsided. (Which is not to say writing those checks has gotten any easier.)

So there I was, taking my daughter to preschool at a time when my high school friends were seeing their kids off to college. I did things almost backward by conventional standards: mar-

riage, divorce, *repeat*, career, baby, and eventually a home reno-
vation involving all-white leather furniture, which many couples
do long before a kid makes such a color scheme impractical.
Nowhere in this picture was there anything like what some other
women enjoy: the nice house in Connecticut or somebody to really
count on. Living and working in the same building, however, has
allowed me to oversee offices in New York, L.A., and Paris and
still take my daughter to school in the morning, greet her when
she returns, and put her to bed each night. Ava is surrounded by a
loving extended family that includes her Italian father, Ilario; her
nanny, Maxine; my dear friends Justine Bateman and Ruth Yang;
my business partners Robyn Berkeley and Emily Bungert; my
parents and siblings; eight cousins; and an entire staff of young
publicists. We are part of a new tribe that is awake and marching,
slowly shifting cultural ideas about what constitutes love and par-
enthood and discrediting the outdated notion of *First comes love,
then comes marriage*, or any other preprogrammed, one-size-fits-all
life progression.

Of course, where I live, everything from same-sex parents
to surrogate moms to single moms to Chinese/German grand-
parents happens to be completely normal. I have gay friends
and a famous pop-star girlfriend who have employed surrogate mothers, the latter because she didn't want to jeopardize
her plastic surgery. I even have a straight male friend I met on a
plane who hired a surrogate when he turned sixty because he'd
never met the woman he wanted to be the mother of his child;
instead, he's raising her with the help of a very capable nanny.
I've done school drop-off in the mornings with mothers who love

their husbands and mothers who hate their husbands and mothers who have given up on their husbands altogether and taken a lover. All around us a whole new world is being born, from single mothers who are *not* urban teenagers in a bind to single fathers, to the interracial lesbians who are every Manhattan parent's worst nightmare in the private school admissions process. (Even as a single mom and CEO, I can't compete with *that* kind of diversity.) This is the new normal.

Now is the time to ask yourself: where do *I* fit into all this? After my devastating abortion at twenty-four, I resolved that I would not give birth to a child before giving birth to myself; at thirty-five, I felt ready. But motherhood is a choice, not an obligation. In my life it has been a teaching, a tangible promise of progress, and a chance to experience totally unfaltering love. I had a baby because I have a lot to give and a lot to learn, not because my husband wanted one or because my parents wanted me to have one or because I viewed motherhood, then or now, as in any way essential to the experience of being female. In other words, not because it was the thing that came next.

Which is not to say that the programmers aren't still hard at work on me. My own mother still calls me up and says, "You know, it was so good to see you. *I just wish you would meet someone,* because God forbid something happens, who would take care of you and Ava?" Reminding her that I'm closer to fifty than thirty-five, I tell her that I can't believe we're still having this conversation. "I know," she'll say. "But you just work so hard, and it would be so great if you could meet someone you could rest into."

I agree that that might be really, really nice, but not what my life is about anymore. If I met somebody I wanted to share my life with *and* that person could be an equal partner *and* my life happened to be at a stage when I could make some time for him, then yes, that would be lovely. But at this point I'm certainly not waiting for anyone else to show up and make me happy ever after. I'm busy scouting out my dream house in the country, making the money to afford it, and making my own happily ever after. Which is why it worries me that most of the girls who work in my office are still operating on a timeline and a set of expectations put in place by their parents or their wedding-obsessed friends who just want them to get married and settle down after a few years of trying on the career thing and have 2.5 children and set about decorating the house. That's fine *if* you feel called to be a decorator, or *if* at twenty-five you've met a man who literally blows your mind in every way. Then you should go for it. Otherwise, examine your real reasons for going along with these expectations. Parents don't want their daughters to come home and say, "I'm going to be a single mom—I'm going to have a baby! I found a sperm donor. Do you remember my friend Jack who I met in London? Well, he's going to send his sperm over, and I'm going to get pregnant." That's not what most parents are waiting to hear. They are still hoping their daughters will make the conventional choices.

Through my daughter, I now see all over again what women are up against from a young age. In fact, I outlawed Disney movies in our house because I thought they were shitty messaging for chicks. From Snow White to Belle, every woman is damaged until some guy shows up and makes everything okay. *Every one* of those stories involves a guy making a woman's life magical. And the first person to try to push this on my daughter was my mother! "We're not buying into this," I told her, but there was nothing I could do to stop it. By the time my daughter was two, she knew who all the Disney princesses were. She never had any of the toys or movies in our house, but she knew everything. Disney is all-powerful.

I eventually adopted an "If you can't beat 'em, join 'em" attitude about the whole thing. I'd say things to Ava like, "What do you think would happen if Belle didn't meet the Beast? Would she still be living in the castle?"

"No," Ava would say.

"Why?"

"Because it's the Beast's castle!"

"But don't you think maybe Belle could've bought her own castle too?"

SEVEN

YOU ARE THE BRAND:
Normal Gets You Nowhere

Those born on November 13 are generally
perceptive and insightful when commenting
on their times. Regardless of what walk
of life they inhabit, they often make
statements about what is going on around
them that attract attention . . . they tend
to have strong opinions about how things
work or don't work as the case may be.

—Gary Goldschneider and Joost Elffers,
The Secret Language of Birthdays

was a publicist from birth. By age two, I regularly crawled out of my crib and waddled into the living room proclaiming, "Johnny Carson! *Tonight Show!*" and snuggled up on the couch with my parents. Several years later, I attempted to make it into the *Guinness Book of World Records* for swinging. Nobody took me seriously until it was time for lunch and I still wouldn't get off the damn swing; only *then* did I convince my mom to call the local newspaper. By eight, I had moved on to producing actual media-worthy events, specifically block-party fund-raisers for Jerry Lewis's muscular dystrophy telethon each Labor Day. These were no small-time affairs: we staged elaborate talent shows (one year my brother and I performed as Sonny and Cher) and stationed my dad at the barbecue grill to turn out hot dogs for half the neighborhood. I always managed to land myself on the local news for being one of the top fund-raisers for the "Jerry's Kids" telethon. If all this didn't bespeak a talent for producing six fashion shows in a single day, getting my clients featured in the *New York Times*, and even producing my own television shows, I don't know what would have, but no one around me ever connected the dots and said, "Gee, this girl would make an amazing publicist!" In fact, my teachers seemed to think I was just an attention-seeker. "Student's social interests supersede academic interests," wrote one, Mr. Dominy, and my parents responded by grounding me.* In fact, I spent a large portion of my childhood getting grounded for doing things that would later make me a lot of money.

By now it won't shock you to hear that I don't believe the people who raised you will necessarily steer you toward your destiny—or even cheer you on to it. With their own ideas about where your life is going, your parents, relatives, and teachers might not be looking for clues that point to other outcomes for you. What might become, in the right context, an important part of your later success may seem like nothing more than character deficiencies or annoyances to them. This is why you need to appoint yourself manager of your own personal brand.

It's not enough just to listen to your inner voice and ask yourself the hard questions about who you are and what you believe. Eventually you need to get strategic about refining and communicating to others who you are and what you believe if you want to succeed. In other words, now that we've dealt with the inside, you need to get real about the outside. Personal branding

* Many years later, after I became a successful publicist, I sent Mr. Dominy a copy of my tax return.

is about figuring out who you are and what turns you on and then *monetizing* it.*

I always laugh when I'm in L.A. and see the huge sign on top of the Beverly Center that reads: DON'T BLEND IN. The truth is that most of us are trying to do exactly that. But if you think about it, the people who are actually making a difference in the world are people who are *not* like everyone else. The best brands stand out. Think about Virgin Atlantic founder and CEO Richard Branson, for example, who is definitely not your typical business guy, or Oprah Winfrey, who is nothing like other talk-show hosts, or the late *Harper's Bazaar* editor Liz Tilberis, a woman famous in the fashion industry for being nothing like most editors-in-chief of major fashion magazines—she had a heart! I believe these people became successful because what they were selling was authentic and consistent. They found jobs that aligned with their skills and passions, and they brought their true selves—idiosyncrasies and all—to work, day after day after day. Take Andre Leon Talley, *Vogue*'s witty, voluble editor-at-large who, despite looking and acting nothing like your average brittle and aloof fashion editor, has been dashing around New York for years in floor-length capes—he is one of the most respected and recognizable faces in the industry. Or look at Grace Coddington, Andre's quirky and opinionated redheaded colleague at the magazine and the breakout star of *The September Issue*, the documentary about *Vogue*. My daughter's pediatrician, Dr. Cohen, is an adorable French doctor who wears Paul Smith suits and makes house calls on his bicycle.

* The Mother herself was a big believer in capitalism. She said that money is ruled by darkness and it's our job to claim it in the name of the Divine.

Every cool mom below Twenty-third Street is dying to get her kid into his practice. Why? Because he's a cute French guy in a Paul Smith suit who shows up on a bicycle, and what's not to love about that? Of course, Dr. Cohen also happens to be really good at what he does, which is key. No one would care about Andre Leon Talley's fabulous capes if he weren't an amazing writer. In some ways, being yourself is a luxury: if I was a horrible publicist, perhaps I wouldn't feel so comfortable showing up to the office without makeup or a blow-out.

Everyone is selling something these days, and if you don't have a clear point of differentiation—something that makes you special, unique, effective—you won't get far in fashion or in any other competitive industry, and you certainly won't succeed as an entrepreneur. All celebrated brands have a point of differentiation. Gucci is selling a black, chic, Italian aesthetic, while Dolce & Gabbana is selling lace and rock 'n' roll and Ralph Lauren is selling chic Waspy Americana. It's time to figure out what *you* are selling and how you are going to make people want to buy it.

In thinking about this question, consider your whole self, and don't be afraid to embrace everything that makes you unique. A family member called me one day, upset that one of her daughters had been diagnosed with a mild case of obsessive-compulsive disorder (OCD). "Are you kidding me? That can be an amazing character trait!" I protested. Look at it this way, I told her: Your daughter's shit is intact! She has attention to detail! *That* is a real point of differentiation in today's attention-deficient world! That girl will make a perfect brain surgeon or photo shoot producer;

all she lacks is a good assistant to manage her time and tell her when to move on to the next task.

Your point of differentiation does not need to be edgy or groundbreaking; it just needs to be different, and it just needs to be you. Most people are mimicking others and dressing and behaving as they think they *should*. But people like Dr. Cohen aren't afraid to challenge accepted molds in embracing their own personal style. Why *shouldn't* a pediatrician make house calls in Manhattan in 2010? And why shouldn't he ride a bike? Similarly, why must all female investment bankers wear pencil skirts and pearls and carry Tod's bags? And as long as we're on the subject, why *shouldn't* a publicist tell the truth?

Since I don't like to lie, one of my points of differentiation in an industry full of falsity is total and complete honesty. My pitching style is truthful and nontraditional; some might even say it's a bit unprofessional. But I get results because I'm saying something different than the dozens of other publicists who call a journalist on any given day. I'm not just doing things the way I was trained to do them or the way everyone else does them. Let's face it: as a brand, adequate and normal will get you nowhere.

How do you find your point of differentiation? The first step is to stop trying to convince yourself—and letting others convince you—that you're something you're not. If you don't like sick people, don't become a doctor. If your idea of a horrible day is fetching coffee and picking up dry cleaning, *don't* go into fashion. On the other hand, if you hate whiny, complaining men, think about becoming a dominatrix, because you'll make a fortune!

This all goes back to the absolute necessity of following your dreams. If you don't know exactly what fits into your life and what doesn't, the best way to figure it out is to follow your inner voice away from what feels wrong and toward what feels right, whether that means moving to New York City on a whim at twenty-one, quitting your accounting job at thirty-five to be an actress, or ditching your job in fashion to swim with dolphins in Hawaii. These experiences won't always take you on an express train to your true purpose and calling in life, but they'll teach you lessons you're supposed to learn. Perhaps these experiences will move you closer to your destiny by revealing that you're *not* in fact meant to be an actress and that what you really want is to start your own fashion line. Most of the girls who show up in my office eventually find out that they are *not* in fact indie fashion publicists. Some have learned that they were designers or stylists instead, and for others the New York fashion world may have revived a dream of going back to school to study anthropology.

Once you have set out on this intuitive journey of dream-inspired self-discovery, you must eventually *focus*. When you find something that feels right, concentrate on refining your skills and educating yourself about your chosen field. Commit to it. You don't have to do it forever—some people are meant to pursue several dreams in a lifetime—but doing one thing well will open doors for you. A plant won't grow as high if it's reaching toward five or six suns, just as a great publicist never works on fashion, beauty, pharmaceuticals, and nonprofits all at once, and an internist doesn't try to also be a cardiac surgeon or a gastroenterologist. Successful people, and compelling brands, are usually highly specialized. They do *one thing*, and they do it in a better or more interesting way than everyone else.

I found my professional niche early, thanks to my willingness to uproot from Syracuse and follow my inner voice to New York. Still, after I sold my PR business several years later in the wake of my divorce and found myself reading tarot cards on Venice Beach, I briefly tried to convince myself that maybe I was not a born publicist after all, but a rock star. This detour taught me that even when a career looks perfect to others or seems perfect on paper, it can still be the totally wrong choice for you.

It all began in 1995 when, high on my newfound spirituality, I ran into an old musician friend from New York named Sean Dinsmore. "Oh my God, you seem so different, what happened to you?" he gasped. I had begun to cultivate a great bohemian look that bore no resemblance to my former label whoredom or my future all-black palette. But it was more than just my look that had changed. I explained that I had gotten into meditation and the Universal Mother*. Fascinated, confused, or both, Sean invited me to visit him in the studio in Hollywood where he was recording a demo. I went, and before I knew it I was lyricizing spontaneously over one of his beats. (The only way to explain this sudden surge of musical inspiration is to say I was *very* relaxed in those days.) Sean recorded me and turned it into a song called "Conversations

---

* I really can't explain the Universal Mother in words. If we sat down and held hands together in meditation as women, we might be able to feel her truth, wisdom, and power. But no alphabet will do her justice, though people have tried over time: Mexicans call her Guadeloupe, the Christians call her Mary, the Egyptians call her Cleopatra, the Greeks call her Athena, the Buddhists call her Tara, and the Hindus call her by several names, from Lakshmi to Durga.

with a Groovy Girl." He then started shopping his demo. When he called me a few weeks later, I asked him if he'd gotten a deal. "No, but *you* did," he said. I was incredulous. But it was true: Atlantic Records wanted to offer *me*—a broke, tone-deaf tarot card reader—the chance to work with the renowned producer Richard Perry (who has produced records for Carly Simon, Rick James, John Lennon, Diana Ross, and Tina Turner, among others). I signed a deal for $150,000, and before I could question whether the Goddess was playing a joke on me, I was pulling up at the bank in Beverly Hills in a pair of cut-off Levis and a tank top, my tattoos plainly visible, to cash a check for $60,000, an unimaginable sum of money for me at the time. I remember the bank teller asking me if I wanted a security guard to walk me to my busted Cutlass Supreme in the parking lot. (I refused, certain that no one would look at me and guess that I was suddenly wealthy.)

Despite my spiritually aspirational state, I was down for rock stardom. After all, why shouldn't the Goddess hit the stage? Surely this was a world that needed some transforming, and no one loved music more than me. I knew in my heart of hearts that I couldn't sing, but I was still going to do my best to make the most of this. I'd faked it to make it before. On my first day in the studio, the producer told me to come in on the sixth bar. "What's a bar?" I asked. I could tell he thought it was going to be the longest recording session of his life. But my songs were pretty good despite my obvious lack of singing talent: I chanted seductively over the beats producers brought me, my style part Lou Reed, part Mazzy Star, my trippy lyrics more often than not tied to my recent awakenings:

I was riding through the cosmos,
Deep in outer space,
Trying to get a grip on this thing we call the human race,
Rat race, out of place,
Krishnas calling out, don't you hear your name?
Darkness keeps on dancing, it never stays the same,
Yes the Mother loves you and it's time for you to know,
Heaven is a comin', it's a souled-out show.

When my album was done, I learned that being a recording artist is not just about making the album; it's about touring, and as cool as that might sound, if you're not looking to get laid or get high, it is one hard job. I was in a committed relationship at the time with the actor who would become my second husband, and the tour lifestyle just seemed tedious and repetitive. It quickly became apparent that I'd been trying to squish myself into a box I didn't fit into. Believe it or not, I'm kind of shy, and I didn't like the kind of attention I got up onstage. In my former career, I'd been communicating and had had actual things to say. Now I was just getting on the bus every day to travel to the next middle-of-nowhere town and wait for sound check before crashing in a depressing hotel. Everything about this just felt wrong. Which is why, despite the money and the promises of fame being heaped on me by my slick representatives at the record label, I admitted to myself and everyone else that I was not a rock star.

My friends at the time were shocked. After all, who doesn't want fame and glamour and money? But I already knew that things that seem perfect rarely are (my first marriage and my first life in New York, for example) and that, in fact, these things can destroy you while you're wrapped up in their supposed perfection. It doesn't matter how glamorous or lucrative a career may seem from the outside; if it's not the path you're meant to be on, you will never be happy or fulfilled doing it. I'd gotten many things wrong in New York in my early twenties, but I had one thing right: I *was* a publicist, and a communicator. Which is why, when the Wasteland came calling not long after I ditched my record deal, I jumped back into publicity with both feet. The rest is history. My distaste for routine, my need to communicate with people on a constant basis, my inability to shut up, my love of language and words—these things are the strengths of my brand as a publicist. And in refining that brand over the years, I've managed to incorporate not only my personal traits but my values and spirituality.

I'd describe my brand today as renegade, strategically kooky, ballsy, bohemian, intuitive, ruthless, and loving. An essential quality of my brand is that people who don't know me often just write me off as a crazy bitch. But *am* I? Everything I do is very well thought out. Sometimes I speak in a loose-associative manner, stunning people and entertaining them into giving in to what I want, even if they have no idea what I'm saying. Other times I might spew a stream of words at someone, going on and on and on until the person just surrenders in fatigue and agrees with me. "Hi, I'm just calling because we're going to need an extra $20,000 for the budget, we've been talking about this $20,000 for two weeks now, and you and I have both probably *already* lost $20,000 individually fighting over whether you're going to give me this $20,000, maybe you just give me the $20,000, and if it doesn't go exactly as you expect it to I'll pay back the $20,000 through some other part of my budget, what do you say, can I have the $20,000?"

The look of my brand, which came later, is also more deliberate than it may seem, and it too was established by moving away from what felt wrong for me and toward what felt right. I started wearing black not because I'm purposefully cultivating a hard-edged image, but because I just happen to look terrible in color! After years of honest appraisal, I realized that black jeans and a comfortable black T-shirt with my hair pulled back and shades suits me best. I now own this look, and it's as much a part of my brand as my pitching style.

In defining the look of your brand, whether you work in fashion or not, remember that there is a danger in trying to create your brand from the outside in. How many girls go into salons every day and say, "I want Jennifer Aniston's hair"? Jennifer Aniston's hair has made her stylist, Chris McMillan, a huge star. Instead of creating an internal sketch, we spend half our teenage years cutting pictures out of magazines and pasting them on our bedroom walls, cobbling together a collage of how we want ourselves represented. If you're lucky enough to be reading this book and contemplating these questions, let me ask you: How do you want to present *your*self? Rather than present someone else's self (*How can I look like Reese or Cameron?*), what is *your* idea of sexy?

These are hard questions. It's much easier to just go with the blond bob and the right bag. Most women by the time they're thirty-eight get their hair frosted and wear running sneakers and signify to the world that they're hunkering down for the next forty years of misery. On the other hand, I believe that the people we perceive as having great individual style have found things that represent their unique inner world outwardly. They're in their truth. They've done the work, and they know who they are and what fits on them and what doesn't. This is why my amazing green, turquoise, soft mauve, black, and white Pucci dress, which I absolutely *love*, is something you will never see me wearing.

People like to know what they're getting when they buy something, whether they're consumers, clients, or employers. At this point, my brand is so well articulated that when I *do* dress up, my clients get scared—they don't know what to think! Backstage at the Chado Ralph Rucci fashion show in New York in February 2009, reeling from my firing by Yigal Azrouel over the Ashley Dupre affair, I wore a purposely sedate Margiela black pencil skirt, a cashmere twinset, and a Burberry coat. Ralph, a new client at the time, was shocked when he saw me: "Are you okay?" he asked. He seemed genuinely concerned. It hit me that my clients don't *want* polished and demure; that's not why they hired me.

Every successful brand has a message, and that message must be painstakingly driven home, in both appearance and substance. It would be bizarre to walk into Tiffany's and see the sales associates putting customers' purchases in red shopping bags because the store's creative director decided that red might be more fun for February. Red just isn't Tiffany! At Tiffany's the service is always imperious service and the bags are blue. In the same way, when a company hires you, remember what you sold them to get the job and be consistent in providing it. And I'm not talking about your wardrobe.

I had an intern a few years ago who came into my office one day and put her head on my desk and started crying hysterically. "I'm about to become disinherited and kicked out of my apartment because my parents won't support me anymore," she moaned. "I'll do *anything* for a job. I'll stay all night. It's the most important thing in my life right now." I gave her a chance, but after three months it was obvious that she hadn't been truthful about her level of commitment. She wanted to leave at seven, she was a big eye-roller, she was the office gossip, and she even turned people against each other. In the end, she quit right in the middle of Fashion Week, screwing over her entire team. Do *not* be this girl. If you sell yourself as a hyper-organized, type A go-getter, that's what you should be as an employee. If you sell yourself as a creative wellspring of ideas, well, you'd better believe your boss is going to want to hear them regularly.

Good brands are authentic, focused, and *consistent*. Of course, your brand will always work both for you and against you: Gucci can never be Wal-Mart in a recession just because it's in the mood to discount; Gucci has to stay Gucci. (In fact, this is why many luxury brands balked in 2007 and 2008 when department stores drastically slashed prices on their goods: the cheap prices detracted from the cachet of the brands.) By the same token, I will never be a demure blonde with a bob in a Chanel jacket who keeps quiet when I think someone is making a big mistake. If that's what a prospective client is looking for—even a client I really want to work with—I have to accept that this is one client who just isn't going to hire me.

Ultimately, no matter how fabulous and well articulated a brand you have, it's of little use to you if you can't sell it to others. I'm talking about getting a job. The best thing you can do for your brand early on is to align it with powerful brands that represent your highest aspirations. This is true whether you're in fashion or heart surgery or sculpture. If you think you may want to work in the luxury fashion business, intern at a prestigious luxury brand like Prada, Louis Vuitton, Cartier, or Hermes—*not* Steve Madden. If you're into avant-garde fashion, you might want to work at People's Revolution or Vivienne Westwood or Bernard Wilhelm. If you're into really high-end, cutting-edge fashion, try Dries van Noten. If you're into art, research the top galleries in the world or contact an auction house like Christie's.

It's the same with your choice of college: if you studied economics at UPenn, you'll get more time from the human resources department of a bank than will someone who went to St. Martin's College of Art and Design in London. On the other hand, if you went to St. Martin's, you'll have a much better chance of getting a fashion position than someone who went to UPenn. Too often guidance counselors suggest the same colleges year after year for wildly different types of people, and that makes no sense. (Which is why you need to seek advice from your own tribal council instead!) Think as early as you can about the network you want to join and the classmates and alumni who will enhance the message of your brand and help you achieve your dreams; be methodical about joining this network. And don't forget about geography: if you see yourself working in high fashion, you should be positioned and prepared to live in a city that offers high-paying careers in fashion, and that is a short list: New York, Paris, Antwerp, Tokyo, London, and Milan. If you are married and living in Chicago and you absolutely never want to leave your husband or that city, it's time to accept that you're probably not going to find opportunities in high fashion and to start thinking about what *else* you may be called to do.

Once you have identified the people who do what you want to do at the highest possible level, start contacting them. You'll be surprised by how many powerful, successful strangers, if you write a heartfelt letter full of good intentions, may agree to be part of your tribal council and give you not only direction but even an internship. If your dream is to work for Ralph Lauren, try sending a letter to *Ralph Lauren*. He may not get it, but you'd be surprised how many times his assistant will, and based on what it says, he or she may be inspired to answer your letter or pass it on to the appropriate person in human resources. Or try calling the main number at Ralph Lauren and saying, "Hi, I'd like to speak to the assistant in the PR department." Don't call the director of publicity; call the entry-level person and ask in a humble way how she got there and whether she would be willing to tell you how to get your résumé into the hands of the right person.

Or send flowers. The assistant might or might not like receiving such a gift, but you're still going to have a better chance of getting noticed than those who send dry form letters making it clear that they haven't done any research into what the department they're applying to actually does. When someone writes me a sincere and humble e-mail or letter, nine times out of ten I'll answer them personally—which often terrifies them—or have someone from my office respond with something like, "Kelly read your e-mail, and here's what she thinks." If it's a ridiculous letter—if a twenty-two-year-old kid who's five-foot-five and fat sends me a picture of himself in his underwear and tells me he wants to be a model—I'm not going to answer it. But a lot of my employees are just people who wrote me moving, persuasive letters in their own authentic voice.

The difference lies not so much in what these letters say as what they don't say ("Dear Ms. Cutrone: If you're looking for someone energetic with a passion for fashion, choose me!"). No one is impressed by a form letter that says, "Dear sir: Upon completion of my graduation in May 2012 . . ." I've never said: "Oh, wow, here's a girl who went to the University of Rochester, had a 2.0 average, and wants to move here from Minneapolis but has no internships. Let's hire *her*!" When it comes to job-seekers who write that they have mad style, and they love fashion because it's glamorous, but they've never even worked in retail or taken a class or interned, I tend to think: *How do you know? How do you know anything* about *fashion?* Successful candidates in my office speak in their own voices—with excellent grammar, of course— but they're not ridiculous in their assumptions about why we'll be so blown away by them.

In creative industries especially, be careful not to let your personal brand overwhelm your expressed desire to learn. The point, after all, is to make people want to work with you. A kid of twenty-two who breezes in acting like Andre Leon Talley is not really going to do it for me.* I'm not a big believer in the Bible, but I do love the phrase "Faith without works is dead." You will be much more appealing to potential employers if you can point to achievements that show how you put your skills and passions to actual use in the world. Instead of spending your summers in the Greek Islands with your family, try spending them at Condé Nast working for *Vanity Fair* or *Lucky*. If I get a letter from a job applicant explaining to me that when she was in high school she saw a fashion show I produced on YouTube and it inspired her to raise $785 for a women's shelter, I'll *definitely* want to meet her. This person is obviously not just someone who is aesthetically inspired by fashion but someone who can connect the dots and think big picture and use her passions to get things done and make a difference in people's lives.

Finally, understand that selling the world—or your industry, or even just your boss—on your brand takes time. As already discussed, you know that the roads of your dreams are not paved with yellow brick; in fact, they may be paved with rejection letters. The people who succeed are often not just the people with the best-articulated brands; they're the people who respond to rejection by brushing themselves off and moving on, again and again. Many college graduates seem to treat paid work as a right,

---

* And as long as we're on the subject, if you come from a really privileged family and your idea of "Oh, that thing?" is a really nice Balenciaga jacket or a pair of last season's Prada shoes, that's probably not the best way to dress for success. Undoubtedly there will be someone in the office who makes more money than you who *still* can't afford to dress like that. The way you express your brand visually can set you up to be liked or to *not* be liked, and it's the first thing people see when you walk into an interview or into your new cubicle after being hired.

not an earned privilege, and expect to be making $125,000 by the time they're twenty-five. I hate to break it to you, but that's not likely to happen these days, no matter how brilliant or authentic you are. If you're trying to get into fashion, you might have to cocktail-waitress at night while you take classes at FIT and send your résumé repeatedly to every designer in town; you'll probably have to settle for a small apartment or, even worse, a roommate; and when you do get a job you'll probably be organizing a closet and coordinating messenger deliveries for twelve hours a day. But these experiences will broaden your empathy, test your courage, and teach you essential lessons about your job and yourself. In fact, if your job still turns you on after these kinds of experiences, then fashion probably *is* the career for you.

I understand that it takes a lot of courage to reach out to somebody who has made it in his or her field. For one thing, we are programmed to be terribly afraid of rejection. Most of us grew up being supported and protected by our parents, and suddenly we're facing a harsher world in which we're overlooked at the bar, our boyfriends break up with us, and we're not getting jobs. Often the problem is not that parents didn't encourage their kids to dream, but that parents were so encouraging that those dreams became their children's expectations.

Ultimately, if you're doing what you're meant to do—if you're in your truth—doors will open for you. I see it in clients like Jeremy Scott, who uses fashion to express his one-of-a-kind pop-art sensibilities, and friends like Mary Ellen Mark, who has revolutionized black-and-white photography. Jeremy and Mary Ellen are great talents, but they're also relentlessly themselves;

they are the best guardians and defenders of their own brands. Like them, I believe that I'm not just receiving teachings and progressing as a human being in my chosen field; in the end, I'm giving the best I have to offer to the world.

One more thing: don't think that creating and promoting your brand is a six-month program. I'm forty-four years old, and I continue to build my brand. The good news, however, is that my brand is much more powerful than it was when I started. I'm now able to use it to help everyone from interns to emerging designers to the charitable causes I care about to flailing large corporations that need an infusion of People's Revolution energy.

There are many temptations along the way—from the allure of star power and elite associations to the temptations that come in the form of sex or money. But even when your wallet or your need to be on a VIP list is calling you, stand strong and remember what your brand is about. As I've said before, the devil always comes looking good. Take Donald Trump. Many years ago, while toiling day and night as one-half of the boutique PR firm Cutrone, Weinberg & Associates, I had the chance to add considerable luster (not to mention financial oomph) to my client roster by signing Trump. It all started when he invited Eartha Kitt, our client, to perform at the Plaza Hotel, which he owned at the time. This being the Plaza, my partner Jason Weinberg and I pulled out all the stops, inviting a bicoastal troupe of glamorous friends like Virginia Madsen, Mary Stuart Masterson, Robert Downey Jr., Alek Keshishian (who directed Madonna's *Truth or Dare*), and the band Dee-Lite, whose hit at the time was "Groove Is in the Heart." As I mingled in my Randolph Duke pantsuit that night,

Trump himself walked right up to me. "I've been watching you work this room, and you're fantastic," he said. "I'd love to have a meeting with you. Here's my card, please call my secretary Norma." I nodded, stunned, but Jason, who was standing next to me, could hardly contain his excitement. The next day when I arrived at the office, he asked me if I'd called Trump yet.

"I'm not calling him," I replied. "I don't want to work with him." Trump had recently taken out an ad in the newspaper defending the innocence of his friend Mike Tyson, who was facing rape charges, and suggesting that Tyson host a fight to benefit battered women. I found the whole thing disgusting, but Jason found my moral outrage expensive. "This is ridiculous. You'll put us out of business!" he argued. And so I gave in.

Trump's penthouse offices on Fifth Avenue had intimidating panoramic views of the city, and Trump himself, then at the height of his powers as a newsmaker, was youngish, handsome, and impeccably groomed in a pink shirt and pinstripe suit. "I've worked with PR people for a long time," he said when we sat down, "and I feel like you're really different. I'd like to ask you a few questions to see how you'd handle certain situations." He told me that he was going to say a few names and that I was to answer "hot," "very hot," or "hot hot." The first name was Ivana, his newly ex-wife. "She's hot," I said honestly. "Why isn't she *very* hot?" he asked. "Well, she hasn't been away from you long enough for us to know how she's going to do on her own," I explained.

Then he asked about Marla Maples, his blond, Georgian, aspiring-actress lover. "She's not *even* hot," I said. "Why not? Why isn't she hot?" he inquired. "Any girl who throws a shoe at you in a hotel lobby is *not* hot," I replied.

Finally, Trump asked me about himself: "Am I hot, *very* hot, or *hot hot*?" I thought about this and then replied, "Barely hot." "Why would you say that?" he said, incredulous. "Anyone who would suggest Mike Tyson stage a benefit boxing match to raise money for battered women is disgusting, and you should be ashamed of yourself," I said. He stared at me and said, "Well, I guess we don't have anything left to talk about today, do we?" I thanked him politely for seeing me, and I left.

Back at the office, Jason was practically buzzing with excitement. "How did it go?" he cried. "Not very well," I admitted. "You *didn't* bring up the Mike Tyson thing?" he gasped. I slowly nodded my head, indicating, guiltily, that I had. I knew what Trump could do for our business, but everything in me intuitively balked. This was not who we were as publicists. If doing PR often requires losing your dignity, I was *not* prepared to also lose my integrity. Trump might have been a godsend for our bottom line, and he himself might also have been one of New York's most recognizable and well developed personal brands, but I still didn't want that brand anywhere near mine.*

---

* I never saw Trump again after that. That's the genius of New York: it's four miles long, I attend events several nights a week, and I haven't been in the same room as Donald Trump in over twenty years.

EIGHT

IF YOU HAVE TO CRY, GO OUTSIDE

The details of your incompetence
do not interest me.

—from *The Devil Wears Prada*

My friends and I joke that I look like a home-wrecker—the person who's going to fuck your husband and eat your cat. Au contraire: I am a woman's woman. One of the things my job has taught me over the years is that I love knowing and working with women. I firmly believe that each woman is a goddess and that deep down inside herself she knows it. I'm known in my industry as an outspoken ballbuster, so my new employees are often shocked to find a certain level of intimacy in the People's Revolution offices. We play music, we laugh, and we dance; we work, we scream, we destroy and rebuild. (These new employees often face a barrage of questions from friends about whether I'm really a bitch and how many people I've fired. "She's a mom!" they reply. "She makes us cupcakes!")

Still, at the end of the day I'm not in the PR business to make friends. No matter how casual I may seem in the office sometimes, I fundamentally believe in grooming the next generation of women to *win*, not in trying to become their friend. My business is a boot camp, baby, for fashion bitches! And as happens in any boot camp, we have plenty of dropouts and plenty who just can't cut it. Get ready for a no-bullshit, to-the-point instruction manual for the real modern workplace that details the unspoken rules you must know to pole-vault forward on your sword of truth, light, and ambition and not get stabbed by it.

MAMA WOLF SPEAKS

By now you know I love the Goddess, but I run my office with the mentality of a more earthbound but still highly mystical creature: the wolf. To my employees, I'm Mama Wolf—I lead the pack. As PR girls in the New York fashion world, we're roaming a brutal wilderness, often fighting for our survival, and I'm here to hunt, teach, and protect, not coddle. Fashion may be beautiful to look at, but the truth is that it's kill or be killed out there, babes.

It's important that everyone understand their place in the pack and contribute accordingly to its success. Like my partners, Robyn and Emily, I am unapologetic about using titles, emphasizing seniority, and acknowledging how much time each person has put in relative to the others. I tell my girls that they should have a sense of entitlement that reflects their title, and I believe this is true regardless of where anyone works. If you're an assistant, you're entitled to *assist*. If you're an associate, you're entitled to *associate*. If you're a director, you're entitled to *direct* and to have all the privileges and responsibilities that go along with that function. It won't surprise you that when we order catering during Fashion Week to sustain us through the long nights we spend in the office seating shows and putting out fires, Robyn, Emily, and I always eat before the midlevel team, which eats before the assistants, who aren't allowed to touch the food until the rest of us have taken what we want. The senior team brings in the clients, after all, and the clients pay for the food. (Like wolves, we share our kill with our children.)

Many young people seem to think they're above the small tasks that make our office—or any office—run efficiently. I've been shocked at how many graduates of expensive, private four-year colleges cannot take phone messages. In my office, for example, if John calls, I need his last name. A phone number with seven digits requires an area code or a country code. I don't want a message that reads: "Pete, 268-7766." Well, which Pete? What city? What country? Who *is* this Pete? "Oh, he said he's a friend of yours." Gee, that narrows it down!

I can usually tell within the first day or two how an intern or entry-level employee was raised based on how they tackle menial jobs. It's often the best-educated young people, the ones who grew up in wealthy towns and have been given every opportunity, who are unable to properly affix labels to five hundred envelopes inviting editors and buyers to a fashion show. No, it isn't glamorous work, but if you treat it like the utterly important task it is—crooked labels reflect poorly on my clients' businesses and my own, and I won't tolerate them—you'll eventually be trusted with larger tasks. If not, you just may be fired at 2:00 a.m. in the middle of Fashion Week—like three particularly daft assistants in my office two years ago. "Thank you very much, that will be all," I said, standing up in disgust after they botched a series of small tasks. "What time should we be here tomorrow?" they asked. "Tomorrow? There is no tomorrow," I said. I cut them checks and asked them never to come back to my office again.

When I open up my office to interns and assistants, I'm not just using them to get my coffee—I'm offering to teach them how to succeed in my business and, if they work hard, give them my stamp of approval. I'm giving them a front-row seat to the workings of my entire industry, helping them to figure out where they might fit into it and giving them the contacts to progress toward their dreams. These are lessons and tools you won't get in a classroom.

If you fail to treat your internships and early work experiences as the amazing learning experiences they are, you sabotage opportunities with the company you're working for *and* you fail to cultivate the friends and mentors who might be resources or might give you recommendations in the future. When I like an intern and I can't hire that person myself, I make phone calls; I go out of my way to help her get the job she wants. And I do this for her not because she has great style or she got my client featured on the *Today Show*; usually I go out of my way to help her because she fetched coffee and affixed labels cheerfully and efficiently and eagerly pitched in wherever she could. In other words, she understood and fulfilled her role in the pack to the best of her ability.

Still, while it's important to be humble and to do even small tasks as carefully as you can, remember that an employer who has invested in you wants your *whole* self at the office, not just your "work" self. When most people are first entering the job market at age twenty-two, they don't yet know how to launch a new product or run front-of-house at a fashion show, and they don't know how to make snap decisions or close the deal at a pitch meeting. What they *do* have is freshness, enthusiasm, questions, creativity, and a point of view. And sometimes it's a pair of fresh eyes that changes the way we do things and alters the course of our business. I would be impressed if an assistant came into my office and said, "I don't know if you know this, but my mom used to own a flower shop, and I'd like to tell you about the way they did their filing, because I think it would really help this office's organization." Knowing your place in the pack doesn't mean restricting your contributions; it just means keeping your entitlement in check.

The assistant or intern who knows her place in the pack also is someone who calls attention to herself, *not* because she's a fun party girl—or because she wears nice shoes, or because she says things like, "I just wanted to let you know that I found some paper towels on the floor and I picked them up and put them back where they should go"—but because of the work she's doing. I'm going to notice if someone's a picker-upper; I don't need to be interrupted and informed that an intern just pinch-hit a janitorial move for me. I'm looking for people who pull their weight in the pack and contribute to its success and vitality without distracting the rest of us from doing the same.

When I say, know your place in the pack, I'm not just telling you to expect fewer privileges than your higher-ups. I'm suggesting that you use the early years of your career, and the cover of the pack, to really learn how to hunt. I am forty-four, and I don't cry

THE *EM*POWERED GIRLS' GUIDE TO DRESSING FOR WORK

[1] No wife-beaters

[2] No cleavage

[3] No belly buttons

[4] No muffin-top

[5] No stilettos or heels over three inches

[6] No flip flops

[7] No gold lamé

[8] *Absolutely* no corduroy

[9] No belly piercings, eyebrow rings, facial piercings, or any other piercings that don't involve an ear

[10] Nothing obviously more expensive than what your boss wears

[11] No Christian Audigier or Ed Hardy, which are forever banned from fashionable workplaces everywhere

[12] No skipping the bra, even if you don't think you need one

[13] No cross-dressing

when a client screams at me. I have enough power and enough experience to tell a screaming client to calm down and get his shit together before he calls me back. But when you're twenty-four and you have a famous designer on the phone threatening to kill you, it can be pretty devastating. Recently, when one of my girls was verbally abused by one of the most powerful talent publicists in the country over a *Gossip Girl* star—the publicist wrongly accused us of alerting the gossip columns that the star had been partying at a nightclub we represented—I stepped in and forcefully (an understatement) put her in her place.

The more successful you become, and the higher your rank in the pack, the more often you have to assume the hunter's role. I'd prefer to spend less time defending my pack and chasing the money we're owed, but I don't always have that luxury. The animal kingdom is ruthless, and when threatened, a female wolf will attack. She's not going to say, "Oh, I'm spiritual, come on in! Do you want to sleep with my mate? Do you want to steal my babies?" She will howl and fight to the fucking end.

Several years ago, we represented a Greek designer who looked like David Hasselhoff and was screwing a married Greek woman from the Upper East Side who was bankrolling his business. Like many clients, he didn't pay his bill. So when the time came for him to pick up his samples—fashion-speak for the clients' clothing we keep in our office to send out to photo shoots—I refused to let them out of my sight. I knew that once the clothes were gone, he'd never pay the bill, and since this had happened more than once in the past, I'd written a clause into our contract stating that I could hold the clothes until I was paid. This angered his lover, a fifty-something former beauty queen, who stormed into my office one day screaming and yelling things like: "*You will not do this! You will not treat him like this! He is a star in Greece!*" She carried on until I told her that if she didn't leave my office I would call 911. "There's someone here trying to remove things that I have the right to keep," I told the operator when she still refused to leave. "I can throw the bitch out the window, or you can come down here and handcuff her and make her leave." When the police arrived, I produced the contract and explained that I had every right to keep the clothes. The beauty queen went ballistic and was escorted out. She soon paid her bill.

Believe it or not, I lose up to $200,000 each year in unpaid bills. That's over $2.6 million in the thirteen years I've been in business. The point is that being Mama Wolf is no joke; that persona is not just about having someone to get me coffee. Sometimes, if you don't eat others, they will eat *you*.

I take great pride in the fact that, despite our hunter's mentality, in our office we do not encourage hurting our own to get ahead, and we do not reward selling other people down the river in the name of competition. If someone is having a nervous breakdown or a panic attack or a drug or alcohol problem, which comes up from time to time, we pull that person aside and say, "We're going to work through this with you." We don't leave an injured wolf in the forest.

Even though I am sometimes perceived as a bitch or a witch, the office atmosphere I cultivate is nothing like the cultural stereotype of striving women clawing each other to death to get the queen bee's job. Women have been taught that, in order to get ahead, we have to be secretive and plotting and manipulative, because a straightforward route to the top hasn't always existed for us, and in many industries it still doesn't. But I don't believe in playing into these stereotypes. We don't *have* to stab each other in the back, we don't *have* to take things personally and break down when we're criticized, and we don't *have* to advance at each other's expense. Being a member of a pack, whether it's a group of males or females or both, is about recognizing each other as assets to the common advancement of the pack and about cooperation as a means of survival. If everyone plays their role to the best of their ability—and if you have a few good hunters on hand—everyone will always have enough to eat. (And ultimately you will also change the makeup of the forest.)

YOUR BOSS

One of the first rules you learn when you start working in my office is that if you have to cry, you go outside. Picture this scene, which has been repeated many times in my office over the years. An intern carrying a $5,000 gown up the steps is so eager to please and be noticed that she doesn't notice that she's dragging it on a hardwood floor that was built in 1898 and has been soaking up dirt and grime ever since. The bottom of the gown is soon black, and rather than being on its way to a shoot with Steven Meisel, it is now headed to the dry cleaners, thus costing my client an opportunity to be shot for Italian *Vogue*. I confess that it is not my priority to convey my displeasure in the sweetest way possible: "Oh, excuse me, honey, if you don't mind, could you please be a little bit more careful?" My response is more like, *"Pick. It. Up. Now!"* I'm concerned about the job our office is being paid to do, not about the feelings of the person who has kept us from doing it.

When my employees make a mistake, I want them to fix the problem as quickly as possible and move on. The last thing I or any other boss wants to hear is, *"Wahhhh, I was just trying to be helpful, wahhhh!"* That's why I officially banished crying to the sidewalk outside. You think I'm a bitch? Fine. Go sit on the street and call your friend and talk shit about me all day. Just get out of my office and stop psychically blowing my vibe and that of the others who came here to make money and be serious instead of being jokers. We may cultivate a purposefully casual atmosphere in our offices, but that doesn't mean we have a casual attitude about work. If we as women want equal rights in the workplace, it's time for us to start acting like equals. You call yourself a feminist? You say you want to advance the women's movement? Then acknowledge that you're no different than anyone else and deserve no special treatment. Haul those FedEx boxes and don't give me or anyone else the luxury of seeing you lose control of your emotions in a professional setting. Once you enter a workplace, you're surrounded by grown-ups, not friends. Your boss is not your boyfriend, and she's not your therapist. She is a person who is paying you to do a job. If you (or she, for that matter) think otherwise, you will be burned.

Still, though she's not your friend, your boss *is* a human being—a little empathy never hurts. Take me, for example. I'm a single mom, I live and work in the same building, and every minute of my day is spent answering the demands of somebody else, from my assistant to my clients to my nanny to my daughter. Because of this, I usually have to eat at my desk while many women at my level treat themselves to uber-chic lunches at the Four Seasons or Cipriani. People call me all day with ridiculous questions like, "Can you get a white horse to a photo shoot in the next twenty-five minutes, because the designer is having a heart attack and will cancel the shoot unless we get a white horse!" If I occasionally snap, "Get away from me, I'm on the phone!" it could be because you're the fourteenth person who has interrupted me since my last latte. Or perhaps the business is taking on more debt and I'm stressed out. Maybe my father is sick. From a very young age women are taught by the culture to regard other women in power as witchy or bitchy, but don't ever take it for granted that your boss is being a cunt because she feels like being a cunt. If you're an oncologist and you've repeatedly had to tell moms with kids that they're going to die, after a while you might seem a little cool when you deliver such news, even if you started out as open-hearted as anyone.

Nobody knows why another person developed his or her individual style. All you can control is how you react to it and how you learn from various situations at work. Even the boss you think of as a tyrant is teaching you how *not* to be a boss, and that's almost as valuable as knowing how to do it. Positive and negative role models are essentially the same: they're both pushing you toward your own voice, your own brand, and your own style. In other words, you can resolve to learn as much as possible from the people around you, and especially those above you, whether they're benevolent leaders or total maniacs.

I am not the kind of boss who micromanages her employees' to-do lists; I was subjected to that early in my career in Susan Blond's office, and I thought it was a huge waste of time. Instead, I hire people who can manage their own time without my help. But working in Susan's office didn't just teach me what not to do. I *am*, for instance, the kind of boss who will not be held hostage for money when my employees get an offer from a competing

PR firm, and that is something I learned from Susan. (If you've been interviewing elsewhere, my view is that you already have one foot out the door and it's not in my best interest to fight to keep you.)

If you work in a close environment and your boss is someone who keeps her door open, don't be afraid to pop in occasionally and say, "Look, I'm going to go out and get a soda, can I get you anything?" Treat your boss like the queen of her castle, but also like a human being with needs who might feel somewhat imprisoned by her life. Instead of thinking, *Why is this person making me go out in ninety-degree weather to get her coffee?* look at it this way: *What must it be like to not have twenty minutes to go outside and walk to get her own coffee on a summer day?* I'm constantly hearing from people, "Oh, what a brutal winter it's been!" and I'm like, "*Really?* I haven't left the office in days!" I was an assistant once too; I know what it's like to struggle to pay your bills and to be at the mercy of someone you occasionally regard as a lunatic. I'm empathetic toward my girls. But I've also gone without paychecks so that they can get paid. Lower-level employees tend to think the boss has made it and has things easy compared to everyone else, but trust me: if she's still working, she hasn't made it.

THE INTER*NOTS*

Recently an intern in my office—I'll call her Anna—decided to entertain readers of her personal blog with stories about her "VERY *Devil Wears Prada*–esque" summer working at People's Revolution. "Interning has taken over my life," she reported breathlessly. "We all work at least 11 hours a day [*lie!*], without a proper lunch break [*lie!*] . . . in fact we are not allowed to eat in the office and we sneak food in the back room." *Lie! Lie! Lie!* She continued: "On a brighter note, I met Kelly today—she was nice but crazy. Last weekend she was hospitalized because her patent leather Prada boots stuck together and she tripped." Okay, that part was true: I'd recently returned to New York in a full leg brace after an afternoon business meeting ended with me flying into the air and smashing down on my hands and knees.*

The veracity of Anna's claims mattered little, however, because she had signed a non-disclosure agreement, or NDA, that prohibited her from writing anything about my company, my clients, or me. The offending post was brought to my attention by another intern, and when I read it, I immediately left a message for Anna on her cell phone (she was off that day). "Hi, Anna, it's Kelly Cutrone, how's it going?" I asked casually when she called me back. "Can I ask you what you're majoring in in college? Oh, really. Are you minoring in law, by any chance? No? Well, maybe you should!" I screamed that she had fifteen minutes to take down her post or I would sue her and her family for all the money they had.

The rest of my interns, taking in the scene from a U-shaped table no more than ten feet from my desk, froze in fear. I believe in an occasional public firing (when deserved, of course) for exactly

---

* I felt silly sitting in the emergency room waiting with people who needed three hundred stitches or were having heart attacks, but I still thought to ask if I could get some basic bloodwork done for a breast reduction I'd been meaning to have. Hey, I am a busy woman, and since I was at the hospital already. . . . Unfortunately, the emergency room flat-out refused to draw my blood and send it to my plastic surgeon on Park Avenue.

this reason. Usually we hide consequences away, in prisons or in rehab. But telling seventh-graders that crime doesn't pay is probably less effective than taking them to a prison to let them see for themselves what happens if you steal or rape or vandalize— now *that's* going to deter them. I certainly didn't go into business thinking I'd need a lawyer to draw up an NDA to protect me from people I'm trying to help by opening my doors and teaching them how to work in my profession. But among the many young women (and the occasional man) clamoring for jobs in fashion these days are those in whom a compulsive need to share everything online is matched only by a healthy sense of entitlement instilled by overinvolved parents.

When I was growing up in the industry, we didn't have hazards like Facebook.* Social media sites may be an increasingly important tool in public relations and other professions—I regularly use Facebook to promote my clients—but for entry-level job-seekers accustomed to using these sites for purely personal reasons, they are fraught with danger. If you're going to post things online about yourself or other people, you have to be aware of how those messages are being followed—not only by your boss, who probably doesn't have time to personally monitor your Facebook page, but by your coworkers. Assume they are reading whatever you post, whether on Facebook or your blog or Twitter.

Even if you're not doing something outrageously stupid like violating an NDA or bad-mouthing a superior, think hard

---

* I now like to say that my Facebook page is a collection of all the people I've been trying to avoid for the past twenty years.

about whether you want your coworkers to see pictures of you drunk and half-naked at that sorority barbecue senior year, or whether you want them to know that you're trying to have sex with the office's accessories director. You're not in high school or college anymore, and if you set out to re-create your family or college friend relationships, you will regret it. Even someone who seems like your go-to office buddy, the one who's in on all the gossip and pointing you in the right direction, might just be steering you toward a crocodile-infested lake. It's best to assume that everything you say and do can and probably will be used against you, and water-cooler talk is now much easier to trace since it's usually available for everyone to read online. Anna made not one but two mistakes: writing about me, and not having the foresight to guess that one of her peers would find it and tell me. When people get fired, it's often because they let their guard down (*or* because they have highly overrated their own importance in the office).*

There's another lesson to be learned here. The more successful you become, the more people will write lies about you on the Internet, both your own employees and anonymous commenters on websites. Your success is an invitation to others to use you as a blank slate onto which they can project fears, aspirations, and prejudices. This has been a harsh pill for me to swallow at times, but ultimately I'd rather be the one *living* the life than observing and making catty comments about it.

* If only lower-level employees knew that my senior staff and I sit around during times of economic peril and console ourselves by discussing how we could still run our company with six people instead of twenty-four. Often we even fantasize about who we'd let go and why.

Maybe what set me off about Anna in particular was her ridiculous suggestion that my interns are expected to "hide food in the back." For the record: I *make* food for my employees. We eat all day long. We order cakes from Dean & DeLuca. Hell, we fly in a chef from India during some Fashion Weeks to cook for the girls! We take food dead seriously. Do not ever suggest that Mama Wolf starves her pack.

GIVE GOOD PHONE

Long before I got my first job in PR, I learned of experiments conducted in the 1950s by a scientist named Harry Harlow. Harlow separated baby rhesus monkeys from their mothers and presented them with replacement "mothers"; some were made of wire, and others were made of terry cloth. The monkeys universally chose to cling to the terry-cloth mothers, even when only the wire mothers had bottles of milk attached to them. In separate social isolation experiments, Harlow's monkeys responded to long periods of solitary confinement by developing lasting psychological trauma, often rocking autistically when presented with scary stimuli. Harlow's results were taken as groundbreaking proof of the basic need for tactile and social contact among higher primates like monkeys and humans.

This study resonated deeply with me at the time, and it informs the way I do my job to this day. I fear our modern loss of human contact. We're addicted to devices and programs that make us feel like we're connecting when in fact we're just becoming more and more isolated and more and more silent. We use Facebook, texting, and e-mail as substitutes for actual human contact; we even call each other's voice mails to avoid actually speaking to each other! And as we get more and more used to electronic means of communication, our senses receive less and less stimulation and our interactions are stripped of their *humanness*. Our tribes dissolve even further. I believe this is what has made us more neurotic and more violent and even more depressed.

My prescription for this dilemma would be to hold one big human square dance, but in the meantime I insist in my business on breaking down the barriers erected by technology and actually talking to other people. I *insist* on giving good phone. As a species, we cannot afford to live on e-mail or to save our intimate communication for only late nights and weekends. Work is where I spend most of my time, as do most people. No two people can establish a high-quality personal *or* business relationship without actually talking to each other. My insistence on calling people on the phone all day has not only helped me form lasting relationships but is now an important part of my brand, and it has played no small part in my success.

It's not that I'm against e-mail—but I do believe that e-mail is a way of documenting things, not *doing* them. It is a great way to reiterate and bullet-point something you discussed with someone, whether in person or on the phone, and it is also a way to reach out to somebody to request a discussion. E-mail was supposed to save us time, but it usually ends up wasting our time. (And we end up sleeping with our BlackBerries under the pillow, as I did for years.) Why do I need to send four e-mails to arrange a dinner? ("Yes." "See you at 8." "Confirmed." "Great.") Why not just tell my assistant to make a fucking phone call?

TOP TEN CAREER DON'TS—OR, HOW *NOT* TO GET A CAREER IN FASHION

[1] Don't send a résumé in May hoping to get hired in the fashion business, as it's the slowest time of year. To increase your chances of securing a top-level job, try January or August.

[2] Do not Facebook the owner of a company or any prospective boss. Or if you do, make sure you have something interesting and out-of-the-box to say that warrants her two minutes; don't just reveal that you went to college and took a résumé-writing class.

[3] Don't roll your eyes. Or if you do, roll with them toward the exit sign and then head out the door.

[4] Don't expect equal rights in the workplace without being willing to do equal work, which includes transporting heavy garment bags, loading and unloading FedEx and UPS shipments, and rolling racks of clothing down New York City's uneven sidewalks. People's Revolution is an equal-opportunity employer.

[5] Don't call in sick when you're not. At People's Revolution, we give employees the dignity of five personal days a year. I instituted this policy so that I would never have to begin my morning listening to sad stories in faux-raspy

In New York, aversion to the human voice has reached epidemic proportions. Recently I called a modeling agent's assistant to make an offer on a supermodel and received a depressingly familiar response. I told the assistant that my client wanted the model to appear at Russian Fashion Week, where they'd pay her $20,000 for one show. "That sounds great," he said. "Can you send me an e-mail?" "What did I just do?" I replied. "I gave you voices about not feeling good enough to make it to the office that day.

[6] If you're going to be a helper around the office and do things you know your boss wants done—for me that means sweeping the floor and taking out the garbage—don't jump up and down and give her a play-by-play each time you finish a task. She knows. Don't underestimate her radar in her own environment.

[7] Do not try to re-create your family at work.

[8] Do not overemphasize your nationality or gender as a way of making a point. You may be a gay man, but you still have no right to wear a skirt and twirl around in the middle of the day proclaiming you're king of the fairies. And if you're from San Francisco and a closet Zappatista, that does not give you the right to play Rage Against the Machine and scream out Che slogans.

[9] Do not think your boss owes you anything other than your paycheck.

[10] And finally, don't cry in the office. Ever. If you have to cry, go outside.

the dates, I gave you the terms, *you're* the assistant, *you* write it up and give it to your boss! *You* fucking write the e-mail!"

The truth is that your communications arsenal is diminished when you're e-mailing instead of speaking: you lose your powers of empathy, tone, charm, and nuance. You also risk failing to communicate entirely. If Paul Revere had sent an e-mail to the colonists alerting them that the British were coming, I would hope he'd also have ridden his horse over to make sure they got it. I hate it when my staffers tell me they pitched a story to a writer when what they mean is that they *e-mailed* the writer and it's quite possible that e-mail is still sitting in that writer's junk box. In fact, there's nothing that scares me more than seeing an office full of people on my payroll, all of whom are communications professionals or aspire to be, sitting there in total silence—i.e., the phone is not ringing and no one is speaking. If we're all being honest, we know that the only reason we text or e-mail each other in the first place is because we're hiding: we don't have time to talk, or we're too shy, or, as in my case, we just don't like the person. (This is a valid use of e-mail: when you really don't want to be intimate with someone and do wish to alienate them.) But when we hide from our fears instead of facing them, we are unlikely to progress as businesspeople or as human beings.

My love for the phone has not only separated me from the hordes of noncommunicating publicists over the years; it has saved my ass repeatedly. One season I had several clients showing their collection at the SoHo Grand, a downtown hotel that I also happened to represent. We realized the Friday before Fashion Week that the hotel's point person had failed to secure the necessary permits from the Building Commission. After a few frantic phone calls, we learned that the commission had put a hold on giving out new permits owing to a few recent building collapses. I reacted the only way I knew how: by making phone calls until I was blue in the face. I figured out the identity of the only man in the city authorized to sign permits, and I set about befriending his assistant, a woman named Veronica. I begged. I prayed. I called Veronica again and again. In my days as a recording artist, I'd written a song called "Veronica Says Hello." I played this for her over the phone (I was desperate). At first Veronica was unmoved; in fact, she kept repeating things like, "No one is *ever* given these things in a day. You're *never* going to get it. These things take months to get." But through some combination of charm and persistence, I wore her down, and she eventually put her boss on the phone.* I told him the truth, speaking from my heart and appealing directly to his. "We have designers who have flown in from all over the world to show at this venue, and because of the negligence of one person they're not going to be able to promote their businesses," I said. "They'll be devastated." He told me he'd see what he could do and hung up. Several hours later, just minutes before 3:00 p.m., when the Building Commission's offices were closing for Labor Day weekend, he called back. "Send somebody down here right now and I'll sign it," he said. I had an intern positioned outside on the street in hopeful anticipation of this very scenario. I hung up the phone and burst into tears of exhaustion and gratitude. (I allow myself a good cry in the office once or twice a year, provided they're tears of happiness.)

Here's another true story. In 2009 two young women from different publishing houses contacted me to offer me book deals. One called me on the phone. I liked her immediately, and we soon agreed to work together. Some months later, after I'd already

---

* This is another important lesson: *always* be nice to other people's assistants.

inked a deal with her imprint, HarperOne, I was going through my junk e-mail folder and found an e-mail from the woman at the other publishing house, offering me a similar deal. I did her the favor of picking up the phone and calling her to tell her never to rely on e-mail as her primary form of communication.

BE THE FIRST ONE IN AND THE LAST ONE TO LEAVE

Most young people who arrive at my office and say they want what I have are not going to get it for one simple reason: they're not willing to do the work. It's mathematics. One plus one equals two. If you consistently show up and do your best, you're going to win the prize. If you do a great job one day and then are kind of tired the next day and don't really feel like working that hard, come in late, and spend the afternoon uploading pictures to Facebook, you're not going to win the prize. Much like building your brand, getting good at something requires consistency and repetition. There is no other way. With few exceptions, you will get out what you put in.

Hard work is a great equalizer. I came from nothing, but from the earliest days of my career in PR I told the truth, I never complained, I was willing to do whatever it took, and I didn't let people kill me in the process. Even as I made plenty of other personal and professional mistakes, my work ethic served me well. To this day, I'm often the first one in the office and the last one to leave, though I make a point of not letting my assistants leave before I do. I don't care if they're done with their work and are sitting there texting their friends. They're going to sit with me. Why? Because I might want a coffee. And if you think that it's my job, at the age of forty-four, to go find a coffee for myself while I'm slaving over a new-business pitch at 10:00 p.m., you're wrong. I'm training my staff to work the hours the job will require. If you want to leave work at six every day, don't work in fashion, and *don't* aspire to be an entrepreneur.

Besides, you'll learn quickly that it's during late nights at the office that the good stuff really happens. Holding a high-pressure job like fashion publicity is like working in an emergency room: maybe you wake up and make a list of the things you're going to get done that day, but then a massive car crash sends in fifty injured people who need treatment immediately, all your planning goes out the window, and by 5:00 p.m. you still haven't crossed a single thing off your list. It's often not until the end of the day that I can stop putting out fires and focus with my partners and senior team on the meat-and-potatoes of the business. It's the time when we argue and brainstorm about where to present a fashion show, who to invite, who should do the makeup and in what color scheme, the music, the seating—all the things that go into creating a show. After-hours in the office is when people drop their guard a little bit; I get to see people like my partners Robyn and Emily, who are more buttoned-up and rigid with their teams, engage in more casual repartee. You can learn a lot during the late hours in an office, from what you want in your marriage to how to put together a great pitch to when you should use a semicolon. When I promote my assistants, I usually take them shopping for a duvet cover and some 800-thread-count sheets because, as a fashion publicist, I joke that their bed will quickly become their favorite place on earth. It's the place where we fuck and where we sleep—two favorite activities we hold close to our hearts, but sadly don't have much time for.

Of course, you also have to learn where to draw the line. Take on as much as you can and soak up as much as you can, but learn to say no when the situation demands it. Don't become the office martyr. I can't tell you how many times my employees have sabotaged projects because they couldn't say, "I need help," or, "I don't understand what's going on here," or, only three hours before deadline, "I'm worried we're not going to meet this deadline." Bosses and owners of companies, who make their living thinking big picture, may not recall how long it takes to execute smaller tasks. Don't be afraid to tell your boss what you need to meet a deadline, whether it's another team member or being removed from another project you're working on. You have to know when to send up an SOS.

No boss wants an employee she's invested in to burn out. Your employer *wants* you to succeed. I don't actually enjoy firing people—well, with the exception of one or two—and most other bosses would probably say the same thing. Think for a moment about what kind of an investment your employer makes in you. You may think the playing field is slanted in the employer's favor since technically the employer can fire you at any time.* It's true that you can be fired if you fuck up or if you just don't work hard or for many other valid or trivial reasons, but as an employee you are also a lot more powerful than you realize.

* This fact of life was one of the reasons I became an entrepreneur, as you'll recall: I didn't like having my fate depend on another person. Nowadays I get fired all the time, but each time it involves only one client among many, not my entire livelihood.

If I hire a senior publicist at $100,000 a year, I have another 30 percent in expenses to pay, including taxes, a BlackBerry, a computer, and unemployment insurance. Hiring this employee is a very costly thing to do, so it's in my best interest if it works out. In addition to the expense, there's the training. Hiring someone is almost like adopting them, especially in a field like PR, which can't really be taught in any college course. I'm not like a chief resident at a hospital acquiring a fully trained surgeon; I'm usually getting a twenty-two-year-old who may or may not have taken a few "Communications" classes in college taught by an academic who's never worked in the industry. I'm agreeing to educate and mentor my new employee and put time and energy into helping her develop the skills that will allow her to interact with my clients as a representative of my company. I want a return on this investment; I'm not sitting around waiting for my new employee to screw up so I can get rid of her and start the headache all over again. All employers are vulnerable to this dynamic, even if they don't acknowledge it.

When my partner Robyn was working too much lately, to the detriment of everything else in her life, I ordered her to spend a month in our L.A. office. I knew that she would never give herself such a break, but I also knew that she needed it. When you suddenly find yourself drinking alone every night or looking in the mirror at vacant eyes, it might be time for you to take a time out too. All of us in this industry, and in any intense industry, need to escape from it occasionally in order to survive. (It's why I have a log cabin in the woods where I retreat every weekend to wear Wellies and row my daughter around a lake in our rowboat.)

There will be days when, regardless of what you do and how much you love it, you'll be disgusted and/or exhausted by it. Anyone at the top of any career has survived their share of mistakes and embarrassments and sleepless nights. I instituted rules like "If you have to cry, go outside," because I've cried. In fact, I've *wailed*! As a young publicist who had not yet learned to control her emotions, I chased people out of my showroom all the time when they offended my client or me, whether by returning a sample item of clothing that had been damaged or by refusing to acknowledge its brilliance. Then, alone, I'd lock the door to my office and break down. Detachment is about learning to have faith in your actions and remembering that you're more than what you do for a living. *And* having a good laugh every once in a while.

When People's Revolution launched the line of the British lingerie company Agent Provocateur in the United States in 2001, we planned an exclusive cocktail party for the press at the brand's new L.A. store. Agent Provocateur made it very clear that the pink color and logo of its brand was a very *specific* pink— Pantone 96C Pink. So I proposed serving perfect Pantone-pink petit-fours with AGENT PROVOCATEUR written on them in black icing. We approached a local L.A. bakery like the really intense PR people we are, barking things like: "Do you understand? This Pantone color has to match *perfectly*! We will accept nothing less than 96C Pantone!" The baker managed to pull it off. So there we were in this elegant, brand-new lingerie store, serving up beautiful little cakes to a crowd packed with celebrities like Dita Von Teese and editors from *Vogue* and the *L.A. Times*. Suddenly I saw

Joe Corre, our client and the owner of Agent Provocateur (also the son of Vivienne Westwood and Malcolm McLaren, incidentally), standing in the corner laughing hysterically, nearly pissing himself. He had already seen what I was about to see: Margot Dougherty, the formidable then-fashion editor of *Los Angeles Magazine*, was turning to me to exclaim, "What a great party!" with black icing staining her lips and teeth. I scanned the room in horror, seeing black tongues everywhere I looked. The icing had semipermanently stained everyone's mouths and lips. I spent half the event in a panic, dragging various fashionable editors into the bathroom under the pretense of showing them "our new vintage wallpaper!" The whole thing was very *I Love Lucy*. But hey, I learned an important lesson: never serve black icing at an event. My mistakes have been some of the best teachers of my life.

NINE

BITCH IS NOT A BAD WORD:
A Call to Arms for a
Return to the Ancient Feminine

The best way of helping others
is to transform oneself. Be perfect
and you will be in a position
to bring perfection to the world.

—Mirra Alfassa (the Mother)

We aspire for a knowledge truly
knowing, for a power truly powerful,
for a love that truly loves.

—Mirra Alfassa (the Mother)

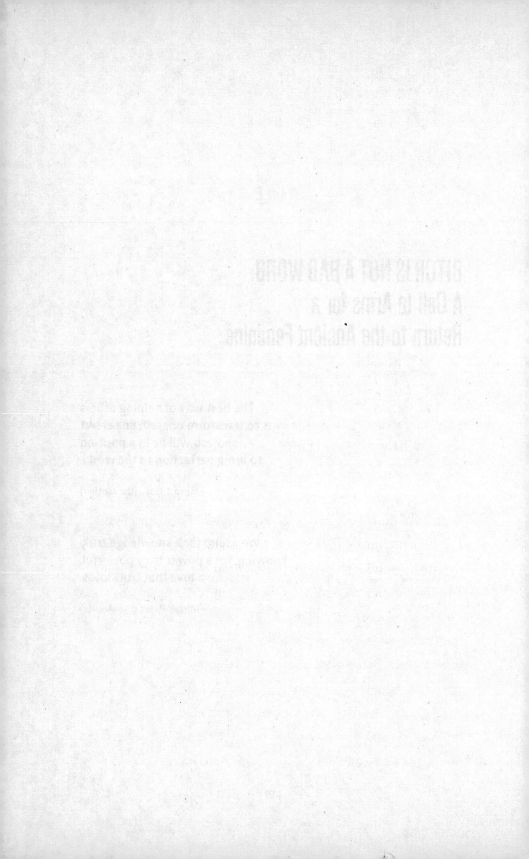

When I was eleven, I became, by sheer force of will, the first female umpire in my small town in upstate New York. I had no great love for baseball, but what's not to love about sitting in the park all day surrounded by cute boys in tight pants and getting the power job of saying who's out and who's not? (Clearly, I already liked to call it like I saw it.) I didn't umpire as any sort of feminist protest; in fact, I was totally unaware that sexism existed! There were no rules expressly prohibiting girl umpires, I didn't know about Title IX, and I also didn't know that women weren't paid the same wages for the same work, that some chose to sleep their way to the top or to make their money from the sidelines, or that female sportscasters were unheard of at the time. In other words, I had no idea that there was anything different about us. But no sooner did I make my first call than the controversy began. Certain families seemed convinced that I couldn't possibly understand the rules of baseball; they booed me, sometimes even shouting mean things like, "Go back to your princess party!" This was when I first understood that some people really hate women in power. What shocked me then and saddens me still is that many of these people are other women. Back on the baseball diamond, the mothers' derision was even louder than the fathers'.

Throughout this book I've encouraged you to embark on an inner journey. But as you move closer to inhabiting and manifesting your true self in all its compassion as well as all its ruthlessness—which will inevitably bring you success in the world, regardless of your job—be prepared: there are people with Uzis waiting on the other side of the glass ceiling who want to kill you. Over the years the playground taunts leveled at me have only intensified. I've been called a bitch, a witch, and a cunt; I've been called a dyke, a troublemaker, and a man (not that I dislike any of those words or types of people). The more successful you become, the more people will project their fears and hatred onto you. This is true for anyone, but it is particularly true of women who dare to speak their minds or assume leadership. Our culture seems to think that women in power are still something new and shocking and we need to be put in our place. But let's face it: women have not exactly been wallflowers throughout history. Powerful women are not an invention of feminism or the twentieth century. Take Cleopatra, who rose to power in Egypt through some combination of smarts and brutality and sex appeal, or Hatshepsut, also of Egypt, who was one of the most powerful women in the world by 1492 BCE. The ancient world and ancient belief systems are full of examples of women who were both fierce and loving, both power brokers and peacemakers. It was only with the rise of more recent religions like Christianity and Islam that women were veiled and screwed into believing they were inferior and powerless and stuck. ("All these breasts are really distracting us from our important holy work; let's make these women cover up, or better yet, let's get rid of them entirely!")

This book is a call to arms (hopefully, arms that have been toned by a trainer, pilates, or Iyengar yoga!). It isn't about being angry women, or becoming men, or going at it without men. Actually, it's not about men at all, even though it's important to note that men have been programmed by cultural forces too and in fact may have it even worse than women right now. (They don't know what they're supposed to do or how they're supposed to act.) But I'm not here to talk to straight guys. Let them build their own army. I'm here to talk to women and gay men.

We have work to do. We've lost all sense of duality in the world, and we're out of balance. In fact, we're dizzy. Women have ascended to the highest perches in many companies and governments, and a single woman who wants to have a baby can get sperm FedExed to her from anywhere. And yet we still have arranged marriage in half the world, and even in the most progressive countries we're taught that as women we should above all be sexy so we can find a guy who will buy us a big ring. Don't get me wrong: if you want to have a vulnerable and open relationship with somebody you love, and you've thought hard about what marriage means to *you*, I think it's great—awesome—if you want to get married. But there are a lot of things we do, or don't do, for other people's reasons. Destructive messaging for chicks is everywhere. It starts with Disney and continues right on up to *Sex and the City*, which, in my opinion, ruined

New York women; there's nothing more depressing than seeing four supposedly liberated girlfriends tromping down the street in thousands of dollars' worth of clothes looking like they just spent three hours getting ready to go out and meet men. Most girls on TV are just saying things like, "Do you think he's gonna call me?" It's not surprising that some people, not knowing how to react when a woman breaks this mold, regress to taunts and sneers. The fact that a lot of the name-callers—at least the ones I've come across—continue to be other women just proves that we believe the lies we've been told about ourselves, and worse, that we're passing them down to our daughters.

The truth is that we're not more or less powerful than men; we are partners with men and have an equally important role to play in the progression of the universe. I believe in a rebalancing between the masculine and the feminine, both inside and outside ourselves. I'm not asking you to become a man; I'm asking you to become a *woman*. To awaken and embrace your true feminine powers and stop relying on men to support you or blow your mind. For many people, the ancient feminine is a veiled concept; the images of power we see around us are usually masculine, from Italian gangsters to—worse—American CEOs. But in Hinduism, for example, the feminine is represented by four different goddesses: one who brings grace and light (Maheshwari), one who destroys everything that is false (Kali), one who creates beauty out of what is left (Lakshmi), and one who puts everything in its place (Saraswati).* I believe that

* *This* is how to be organized.

all of these abilities are latent in every woman. We just have to find and fearlessly manifest them.

Truth be told, I have never seen "bitch" as a bad word. Instead, I see the word for what it is: a reflection of people's lack of creativity and inability to acknowledge and embrace a powerful woman. It's as if the best some people can do is give me a nod by calling me a bitch—in which case, I'll take what I can get! It's fair to say that the true definition of "bitch" is a woman who won't comply. I hope humanity evolves to a place where the word "bitch" will no longer be needed and a successful and powerful woman can just be called "strategic" and "ambitious." In the meantime, all over Salem, Massachusetts—one of my favorite towns, I take my daughter there each Halloween—there are signs that read: WITCH: WOMAN IN TOTAL CONTROL OF HERSELF. If that's what a witch is, then a BITCH must be a Babe (or Boss) In Total Control of Herself.

Ultimately, though, I'm not asking you to own your own company, or to do things my way, or to be a CEO of anything except your own journey in this world. I'm asking you to start the church of *you*. I want you to refuse to pray or play at places that won't let you speak or where your gender has no power. Or, fine, if you really have to go to these places, go with the intention of transforming them. I want you to fearlessly pursue your dreams and your destiny, conscious that you are *not* what you do, listening to your inner voice, refusing to let superficial things define you, asking yourself the hard questions about what you believe and what you will serve, fighting the fears in your own mind, and finally, loving other women in the process.

When we're young, we're taught to compete with other women for what we need to survive: money, or a husband. But if you're going to be ruthless to another woman, you'd better make sure that your intent is pure and doesn't come from jealousy or bitterness or any of the other problematic feelings and fears we're taught to have about each other ("she's a homewrecker," "she's going to steal your husband," "she's younger than you and wants your job," and so on). We need to be open to the concept that we as women have more in common than not; we need to stop thinking of each other as adversaries. I was devastated early in 2009 when I read about women in Afghanistan protesting a law that demands they submit to sex with their husbands at least every four days: many of the people pelting these brave protesters with stones were other women. The goal of our inward journey is to change the world by changing ourselves, but none of us can change the world alone. We need to help each other, or at least get out of each other's way.

It's easy to think that the problem is outside yourself, that it's all Hollywood's fault, or that it's other people who need to change. As a young party girl in New York, I often ended my nights at a club in the East Village called Save the Robots, which was open from two to eight in the morning. It served screwdrivers in Tropicana cartons and cranberry vodkas in Ocean Spray bottles. On my way home to Avenue C, I stopped regularly at a bodega to buy muffins to distribute to the homeless people in Tompkins Square Park. They began to refer to me as the Muffin Lady. But they were also laughing at me under their breath. I was trying to solve *their* problems when I was obviously loaded and going nowhere fast myself. I'm not saying we shouldn't use charity toward others as a way of learning lessons and doing good in the world, but I am saying that the primary work of our own lives is inside ourselves (it's a macro/micro kind of thing). The wars in the world are outward manifestations of the war that rages inside each of us; charity and change truly begin at home.

I've spent years wrestling with what's important in this life. Is it being the hottest, coolest girl, the one with the best job who's having the most fun, or is it escaping to someplace like India and turning my back on the material world to immerse myself in the metaphysical? The truth is that for me, neither of these lives works. They're both invalid. My journey has been about forming an "X" on the spot where the heights of glorious superficiality meet the depths of spirituality. Worldly success and divine transcendence are *not* mutually exclusive. Fame and success will *not* bring you happiness without a deeper knowledge of yourself and a connection to something greater than yourself.

At the same time, contemplating the meaning of life under a banyan tree in India is of little use to anyone. As my guru the Mother said, money is a force ruled by darkness, and it's our job to claim it in the name of the Divine, appointing ourselves trustees of her money. We do not need to be starving monks in order to be holy people; this is over in my religion, and I hope it's over in yours too. If I could wish anything for you, it would be that you could accomplish in one year what it's taken me forty-four to figure out. The world needs you. It needs you to find and fearlessly manifest your true and powerful and authentic self, and it needs you to enjoy the pleasures that are here for the taking. I hope you'll find inner peace and know the abundance of prostrating yourself in front of the Divine. And I hope you'll know other kinds of abundance too, whether it's climbing to the tops of the Himalayas or buying bracelets at the counter at Hermes. Tell them Kelly Cutrone sent you.

KELLY CUTRONE SPEAKS

These are questions culled from my Facebook page, which has become the place where I meet and interact with friends and strangers (mostly strangers) in cyberspace. On October 19, 2009, I asked my friends and fans what questions they'd like me to answer in my book. I received seventy-four questions and picked my favorites.

Do you comb your hair?

I wake up in the morning at 7:30 a.m., take care of my daughter, shower, comb my hair once, either throw it in a ponytail or don't, and then work in several time zones for the next fifteen to sixteen hours. This is how my Amish psycho killer look came about. I don't have nice hair. I don't have hair extensions, and I never will.

Why don't you wear makeup on TV?

Because unlike other people on TV, I am really working. My look has evolved out of sheer survival. I think America can handle the fact that I don't wear makeup.

How do I get an internship at People's Revolution?

We hire for three different periods during the year: January to May, June through September, and September to December. We request that our interns work a minimum of three days a week, and we prefer interns who work for college credit. That said, before worrying about getting your résumé on my desk, I suggest that you first build something that will prepare you for a high-ranking fashion career: other internships, a knowledge of the industry, a knowledge of the city you're applying to work in, and another way to make money while you seek work. Then write a meaningful letter from the heart. Your pitch letter should be something more than, "I love fashion, please help me manifest my dream." Also, check your punctuation. If you're applying to work in communications and you don't know the difference between a comma and a semi-colon, maybe you should invest $50 in having someone who does know the difference proofread your cover letter. Also, do not use rhyming words on your résumé, as in, "My passion is for fashion." This works only if you're applying to work for the estate of Dr. Seuss, Nickelodeon, or the Scholastic Company.

Who are your favorite designers, past and present?

Margiela, Paco Rabanne, Paul Smith (for shades), Commes des
Garçons, Yojhi Yamamoto, Couregges, Dries van Noten, Vivienne
Westwood, Jeremy Scott, Zandra Rhodes, Anne Demuelemeester.

What are the characteristics that drive success in this industry?

Creativity, truth, and commitment.

Do you ever get bored with it? Like wake up and go OMFG WTF?

Yes, at least nine times a month, and sometimes more if I've been
out late the night before.

How hard was it for you to get to this level in your life?

It took every breathing moment of every day I had. But I guess
anyone could say that.

How do you balance your family and free time with your career?

By getting rid of the "I" in the equation. I tend to focus on my
daughter and my career. I live and work in the same building. I
see my daughter every day, and we go away every weekend to
the country. My secret "passion for fashion" is Target.

If you could cast a love-spell on someone, who would it be?
Can I pick more than one? Gabriel Byrne, Jeremy Irons, or Leonard
Cohen.

What makes for happiness in the fashion industry?
If it's happiness you're looking for, I suggest you try another profession.

What happened to curvy women?
I believe it's the consumers who drive the market, not the market
that drives the consumers. I promise you that if 60 percent of society decided that chunky, Rubenesque women were the epitome
of fashion chic, the first people to give it to them would be fashion designers. But society is into the concept of thinner, younger,
faster, better. Look around; they've taken great American litera-
ture and turned it into Twitter.

Who was or is your greatest inspiration?
The Goddess Durga.

Where do you look for creative inspiration?
I tend to look within myself.

Do you like girls?
Once, I was walking down the street and a few canvassers asked
me to give them money for an AIDS charity. I declined, because
People's Revolution already gives money to several charities. As

I walked away, the two canvassers said, "You're our favorite lesbian on television!" Well, the truth is that I slept with a woman once, and afterward I coined the expression, "When push comes to shove, I prefer shove." I love women, but I have no desire to make out with them, have sex with them, or go find a sperm donor with them for my second child.

Do you believe in life after death?
Yes.

Has the work of Andy Warhol ever influenced your work?
Well, I did marry his protégé, Ronnie Cutrone, who provided a wonderful foundation of pop culture knowledge. And Andy did say that everyone would be famous for fifteen minutes. I just didn't think that would ever include me.

Why does everyone in your office have to wear all black?
Let me dispel this rumor too: the kids who work for me can wear whatever they want, except to events. When we go to events, black is the closest thing to a uniform we have. It's not identifiably any one designer. If we go to a Jeremy Scott show, we can't be wearing Donna Karan. So black keeps everyone easily recognizable and looking chic.

Why do you wear all black?
I wear all black because I don't look good in color and because it transitions easily from day to night, which is what my job requires.

What's the best city in America for fashion PR?

New York.

What will the next step in your career be?

I would love my own talk show.

What is your view on the future of fashion?

Fashion will always be important because we have to wear clothes to protect our bodies from the elements while we search for mates. That said, I think the focus will shift to emphasize the items themselves rather than huge collections. I also think that retail stores will change and that clothes will be delivered on-time instead of pre-season. Who needs wool pants from Ralph Lauren when it's 105 degrees outside? The Internet, which has played a part in the death of music, will also take a chunk out of fashion and television.

Are you into witchcraft?

When you go on television, you basically make a deal to empty yourself of everything and let the people who are watching you project everything onto you that they want, whether that be fears and hatred or hopes and aspirations. And then there are stereo-types. With women, three common stereotypes are summed up in the words "bitch," "witch," and "cunt." At least, these are the ones most commonly used to describe me. I kind of like the word "bitch." I believe I'm here to own it. But am I a witch? Frankly, it takes way too long to do all those spells. Witchcraft is outdated.

I like to think or say things and make them happen immediately. However, I do go to Salem, Massachusetts, every Halloween with my daughter, and some of my closest friends are Wiccans.

What do you like to do when you leave the office?

I cook, and I try never to answer my phone.